FROM THORNS to THRONE

Unique Life Experiences to Shift Your Mindset

(Based on True Life Experiences)

DEDICATION

In life, we are Spirits having a human experience!! This ***"experience"*** isn't supposed to look, feel, or sound the same! Same formula?? YES!! We often forget. Right, wrong or indifferent, perception IS everything! As my fellow BEING, your two positions in life are: (1) Making sure You are of SERVICE to others, and (2) The perception of *U* others see is one of love... DIVINE LOVE! We are ALL allotted a small amount of time to show and prove those things. Along the way, I REFUSE *TO* LET ANYONE TELL *MY TRUTH*!! For this, I give to the world, ***FROM THORNS TO THRONE:*** *Unique Life Experiences, Five Key Words to Shift your mindset from the Thorns to the Throne.*

This book is dedicated to my little cousin, *SHAWNITRA LAFAYE*, who left us so soon. Also, in the loving memory of my *great granny, MILDRED, and best friend, AYANNA.*

Red Thornz Blaqk Roze Red Thornz Blaqk Roz
Blaqk Roze Red Thornz Blaqk Roze Red Thornz

CONTENTS

FORWARD

Belief

Trust or confidence in someone or something.

My definition of Belief

My reliance on my gut feelings (first mind) and my ability to execute.

3 Keys to help develop self-belief

1. Face your fears: Please take steps to diminish the obstacles in your way by educating yourself on them.
2. Be prepared to win: You set yourself up for success when you look, feel, and be the part.
3. Cut off negative acquaintances: If you have any doubt entering your inner matrix, get rid of it. You will eventually start to believe the negativity around you.

THORN ONE

I was wearing a light pink dress that flared at the bottom. If I spun around, it resembled a blossoming flower. This beautiful dress set off my big, mahogany and honey-brown eyes. If hit by the sun, my eyes would sparkle like chocolate diamonds; I was a sure compliment to the sun THAT day! As I was swaying at the park, my big brother, Ivonne, helped in pushing me on the swing.

"Kick your legs, DD!" he would repeatedly say until I did it. As I was going higher and higher, I'd look up to the sky with no specific thought in mind; only of me having the time of my life! The warmth of my thoughts wrapped around me like a hug and I began to feel a ringing in my ear. Suddenly, I began to feel an overwhelming awareness, as a sense of control took over my mental activity. I was now watching a movie play in my mind. This sphere of activities included a red van, four adults, and a moving swing. These adults jumped out of the dirty van and started running in a direction with nothing but fury in their eyes. Their speed was unquestionably terrifying. One of the grown-ups was a man, accompanied by two other women. The last to exit the van was a little old lady. She appeared to mean business; the Ring Leader! She opened her mouth and out flew a piece of hell; letters covered in flame, some covered with spells and daggers. I quickly searched her host, and there weren't even an ounce of light in that vessel.

The little old lady nodded. The three adults got the job done, as they snatched and forced three children into the van. This was the last thing I saw in this confusing ass mind movie; a swing that doesn't appear to have needed any help from a human to move it back and forth. But in reality, my entire being felt as though it was traveling through time rapidly. I was forced back to what a six-year-old little girl knew as her life. My mind mushed and my body melted, causing leisure motions of my right hand.

With my tiny, quiet, and peaceful voice, I whispered to Dakota to help me off the swing. Since there were other kids around playing, it was hard for my brother and sisters to hear my fragile whispers. I was sitting there and wondering, "Okay! How the hell am I going to get off the swing?" I wanted to do something else. Maybe go down the slide. "Oh well! I guess I will wait until it slows down."

Suddenly I began to hear a ripple of sound and I looked in the direction from which it was coming. The sound grew louder as the red vehicle with tinted windows approached the play area. At this point, I began to feel like I've been here before. Four adults jumped out of the vehicle and swiftly scooped up three kids as the rest ran. Shrieks of terror filled the sky while all the kids scattered to safety. In the midst of all that was going on, I was in the corner on the swing. "Did everybody just forget about me?" It was like I wasn't even there; almost invisible! Once I could stop soaking my pretty pink dress with tears, my heart was in utter disbelief that all this happened within seconds. I closed my eyes tight and jumped, landing in the sand with my hands and knees buried. I looked up and saw the swing that seconds ago seated me for what I knew as innocent fun, now gliding at the same pace as the wind.

Alone in the park, I picked myself up in a hurry. I briskly built enough adrenaline to run at full speed. Every time I would hear a twig under my feet during my marathon, I would hit the deck and hide in a bush until I felt the coast was clear!

I used my hands to wipe away my tears as it continued to flow. My vision was cloudy and couldn't see how close I was getting. At some point, I became my coach. These were the most extended six blocks of my little life. "Keep Running! Keep Running! Keep Running!" the WILL in me continued to chant—my heart thumping like a sacred drum. I quickly looked back to see if my coast was clear again. BAM! I ran into something, or more like someone. The tear faucets I turned on were distorting my vision and everything was fuzzy. The foundation in my house of consciousness was trying to understand and manipulate the experience I just had, and the confusion was causing my body to react. My brain was trying to recall, summarize, categorize and assign a role. However, this process was cut short as I noticed a man standing in front of me. His build appeared to be very Paul Bunionish. Maybe 10 feet or so. His silhouette gave off a calming aura, and feelings of familiarity embraced me. Need I remind y'all I was six at the time? I was wiping the last bit of my tears with my arm when I made direct eye contact with this man. I knew I must get up from the ground; he knocked me down too.

I rush to be comforted by this man I call Poppa. A child's early years of development are critical; the brain (house of consciousness) grows the fastest from birth to the first eight years. Within those years, a foundation is built. Some of the building blocks include learning, understanding, evaluating, and categorizing feelings, words, and memories. The foundation is also where rearranging and assigning a role happens. The experience, words, or feelings are pushed through to the subconscious part of the mind (house). It is common for the trauma experienced to sound an alarm versus a positive experience. The mind wants to categorize the experience anywhere until we find an honest answer for the role. Then the child's mind stores that information in the subconscious.

The child's guardians, family members, and other care providers' responsibility as their CORE BELIEF CREATORS are to help them develop the right skills to become healthy, independent, and lead successful lives. Exposure to trauma and stress will have short and/or long-term adverse effects. We must detect early trauma to be able to reinforce positive stimuli.

"What's the problem, DeMarie? Where are your brother and sisters?" I began to bellow out the most shrieking whine. "Some people came and took them from the park! Then they forced them into a red van with dark windows, Poppa!" Hard panting while forming the words was difficult. My mind was still trying to find a place to store my traumatic experience. "We've got to do something!" was my cry as I jerked his construction gear back and forth. "Wait, wait, wait...PUGGA!" Pugga was the term of endearment he had chosen for me. "Calm down and tell Poppa what's going on!" He comforted me on the way to the house and made my favorite... lemonade!

I could replay everything from when we got to the park until I ran into him. As I told the story, I could see the temperature rise in Poppa from when he began to shake his feet at a rapid speed, clenching his teeth. To that, he alarmingly paced back and forth. "Those bitches!" he repeated out loud over and over again but to himself. "DeMarie Pugga, can you go to your room, please? Poppa needs to make a few calls, okay?" "Yes, Poppa. It took a bit of effort to climb down from the kitchen table, but I managed.

I didn't make it to my room. I learned from my elder siblings to always peek around the corner to hear what was happening. I believe the first call was to Mommy. Mommy was at work. I gather she would be home soon by the way Poppa spoke to her. I recall sliding down to the floor as I held up the wall with my left side. I sat and replayed the things Poppa had said; maybe I could make sense of this shit! I grabbed my chest, as it was beginning to ache. Just as the words came to me, so did the water faucet.

Like many, my mother fell victim to this crack rock era. At my tender age of six, she met a gentleman named Tony. I don't remember Tony as a child, but the stories I heard as an adult made sense. Tony was a very light-skinned man who was of average height for a man. His hair was very wet silky curls that sat on his shoulders, complimenting his green tea eyes. More so, he had a magnetic spirit. I can see why Paige fell for him. He looked like money. Where I'm from, that could mean he had the bare necessities of life, which he could easily acquire. You never question the HOW. Paige met this guy from one of the many adult parties. Sure enough, Paige caught his eye, and he charmed her with his loud, flashy clothes. With a frame covered in jewels, it made it hard not to be attracted to the things you didn't have. It didn't take long to seduce a young lady with generational curses decorating her neck. It was often louder than the jewels Tony was wearing.

There had been a shift in Paige; something was different. At six, I had no clue a substance could do this to someone you love. Before she was introduced to her *kryptonite*, Paige strived for loyalty, respect, love, and honor amongst her children. She taught us everything she missed growing up with nine brothers and sisters. The BELIEF in GOD was a cornerstone that would cement our trust in The Most High GOD, who isn't tangible if you don't believe. Her childhood had been ruined; the people who were supposed to protect them blinded them with neglect, incest, and physical and emotional abuse. The absence of love would send them on a spiral of sex, drugs, gangs, and, most notably, loss of self.

An invisible band aid was just what Paige needed to maintain and suppress all of what brought her to feel unwanted and appalled by her past. It kept her numb to life.

"I bet your mama and your sisters came and got them! I hope you're fucking happy."

I could hear Poppa's footsteps in my mind, and I knew it didn't mesh well with my gathered thoughts. Immediately, I snapped out of it. I ran to my room and laid down to cover my tears. To my little self, Poppa was a silk chocolate brown with an afro and goatee. He had what he liked to call K9 teeth, and his hazel brown eyes made him radiate. He was a man with a good build. Thanks to his career choice of construction. To top it all, he also had a deep stern voice; when put to use, it gave off sound waves and had lightning attached to the words. He spoke with certainty and boldness that held no feeling. But when it came to me, he gave it all he could to show me emotion in his words. I loved him for that effort! The aura he had around him was blue and calm.

But his voice would still send wrath.

Sometimes Poppa spoke to me as an adult; I didn't understand everything, but he always said I would understand later in life. Then Poppa walked into my room. I had just flopped on the bed with parts of my body dangling down. He would sometimes call me DD. It was his way of getting my attention - usually, when it was time to sugarcoat things or when he had something up his sleeve. "DD", he attempted to whisper. His attempt was still a thunder that crept up my back and grabbed the hairs on my head. It forced me to turn in his direction and look him in the eyes. "Things aren't working out with your mother and me."

"I am angry, hurt, and disrespected by your mother and her family. I won't let anyone or anything separate us! Do you hear me?" This time Poppa's words would grab my ears to ensure I was listening. "I'm going to fix her and them."

Poppa took me to my great aunt Sugar's house. Her house was on the same property right in front of ours. He did so when mama wouldn't come home, and I didn't mind. Auntie Sugar operated a daycare from her home. She was close with all the children and their families. We called her Nana, a grandmother figure. Poppa kissed my forehead and told Nana not to let me go with Mom if she showed up.

I grabbed my favorite blanket. Before I closed my eyes, I prayed to the Lord above to take my soul if I should die before I wake. My prayer was equivalent to a mother singing a lullaby for her baby. I would wake up at 7:00 am daily, the time Poppa came home from work, which was also the time Mommy would leave for work. I thanked GOD for keeping me safe. I washed my face and brushed my teeth.

I loved to run straight to the dining room area of Nana's home, where three windows stood - two square windows on the ends and one long rectangular one in the middle. Underneath these windows were two chairs under the smaller windows and a round tea table under the long rectangular one. Both the chairs and table had all white silk with lace patterns on them for a table topper. Nana had a teacup set that was of the most delicate China. This window was designed to meditate, hold social conversations, drink coffee, etc., you name it. Nana would do it right there in that window. One could guarantee that Nana was in the window if you stopped by. At times, I could see Nana talking to a man sitting across the table, laughing and having a good time. I would always see this man whenever I was outside with my cousins, and I would ask one of them, "Who is that man talking to Nana?" The rebuttal was always as if I was crazy. "What are you talking about, DeMarie?" I dropped everything I was doing. I ran up the enormous rock stairs, followed by twenty steps to get to the front door.

I hit the corner to the left. Nothing! Nana was alone. "What's wrong with you, girl?" "Nothing. Nana, who was sitting in that chair talking to you?" She always smiled and said, "Go back outside and play, baby." She left me quiet and confused because she never answered my question. I got back outside to play. Two hours of playing outside, we were called back inside for dinner. After dinner, it was time for bath; I wouldn't say I liked bath time. Uncle George's room was next to the bathroom.

Uncle George was disabled. He liked to yell and say thunderous cuss words. GODDAMMIT and SON OF A BITCH were a few of his favorites. The sporadic words that came from his room always startled me, but not as bad as the knowledge of his cold presence, which gave me goosebumps in the tub.

When I got to the table, Nana was at the window. She was humming a lovely tune sure to quiet the fussiest baby. She drank tea as she watched the sunrise. I struggled to get up in the chair to have a cup with her. I had a passion for her melodies but this time, I could feel her songbird singing its song to me. It was almost like it was telling my story. At the same time, it nuzzled my heart and mind. When I turned to Nana after looking in the window, she smiled at me with mixed concern and possible sadness.

It was 9 o'clock, and my mother hadn't come around. Poppa also didn't make it in from work. I heard Nana on the phone saying, "I knew she would use this as an excuse to run off. That Paige lost it this time! Yeah, her mother took the other three kids. She is also fighting for custody. Uhhhhh hhhmmmm!" She spoke in her best gossiping voice. "Rodell is on his way to the courthouse to fight for DeMarie. I pray she hasn't lost complete willpower to fight for her kids and sobriety." "If she doesn't come by tomorrow, you can bet your bottom dollar that girl won't be back!" Aunt Sugar carried on. Those words would ring with an echo in my mind; Mom's not coming back. I was seated in the kitchen eating a bowl of Cap'n Crunch, and I felt a knot in my tummy that wouldn't go away for years!

Time waits for no one. Days will keep passing, seasons will still change. I was hopeful Mommy would catch up. I was almost seven at the time and I wanted her to see how big I was. I wanted to tell her I loved her no matter what was going on and that I had forgiven her.

Yes, Mommy didn't return and Poppa got full custody of me. Everyone around me did enough to comfort me and keep me happy. However, Poppa thought I needed a new mom. At the time, I didn't know I needed a new mom. I tried very hard to keep good memories of Paige. How could I? People would say, "What were the most offensive, bad words people thought to speak?" These words overpowered the loving words and things I could remember about her, including her scent and appearance.

I always like to be alone. I found comfort in silence—no one to judge me or my situation. There was nobody to speak ill and let the air out of what memories I did have. When I was alone, I could just be me. I also was reticent, as church mice whisper. I mean, you couldn't get as much as two words out of me, on top of not being able to make out a word. I was no longer that cute baby girl that everyone felt her sorrow. Their true colors were beginning to show. I am the product of Paige. How could I become anything more than what she is? Poppa had gotten to a place where I was almost a burden to his single lifestyle, so I stayed on my knees. Without complete understanding, I brought it all to Jesus because I knew He will ensure it got to GOD. The words began to flow from the bottom of my soul. Lord, I am sorry if I have been a bad girl, or maybe I cursed too much. I need you right now, Jesus. I am alone in this world. Nobody wants me around, so all I have is you, Dear Lord. I trust in and rely on you, Jesus, that Paige will return and that you will never leave me. Amen.

More often than not, I would wake up to early morning rain. In my mind, I felt like the rain was GOD's way of throwing my tears back at me. Deep down in my soul, I felt like a motherless child! Even though I knew Paige was alive, the yearning became stronger. I was still so innocent of the world that it had not yet consumed me or changed my thoughts about life. I came home from school one day with an idea I thought was sure to work. At GREENWOOD Elementary, first graders were learning to write pen pals. My great idea was to write mom a letter; indeed, the friendly old mailman we had for years could get this letter to her. I finished my homework and did everything I could to help around Sugar's. I even volunteered to go first, counting to one hundred, so I won't be interrupted when I sat down to write. Here goes nothing…

Dear mom,

Can you just come home, mom? I promise to keep my room clean. I won't say cuss words. Please, what did I do? I will never believe those guys. Mommy, I never wanted to think that those things are true, but so much time is fading I feel like you're slowly slipping away!

Love,

DeMarie.

I colored the letter with red hearts and drew a picture of Paige and me in our Sunday best on our way to church.

I raced around the house, looking for an envelope. When I found one, I became overjoyed and excited that I had such a fantastic idea. It was too late in the day to catch the mailman, so I had to tell him I had a special delivery. I walked down the stairs to the mailbox, put the letter in, and pulled the red handle up. As I pulled up on the red handle, I received a jolt in my mind that would change what reality was supposed to be. I saw the mailman talking to Nana (Aunt Sugar) and handed her a large mail stack. They both appeared to have aged just a slight bit. The vision felt natural!

I was at the window watching this take place. Suddenly, this dreamy reality disappeared and I was back in my comfort zone with things I knew to be authentic, like the sound of wind in the air and birds talking back and forth. The fact that I was standing in front of the mailbox helped confirm my reality! Dammit! I couldn't remember for the love of me why I was standing in front of the mailbox holding the red handle. I assumed that I must have appeared to be disoriented and confused. Hell, maybe even lost. I thought to open the mailbox, and there was my envelope. I knew it was mine because I colored it with balloons and a smiley face sun, the most fluffy ass clouds an almost seven-year-old could make. It was the moment I was looking for, a minute of sense of fullness. Something that helped me remember why I was standing there. I took off running into the house filled to the max. Not quite sure with what, but all I knew was that my cup had runneth over.

Later that night, I laid in bed so full of questions I needed answers to. Such as, "Where in the fuck do we come from? Where does GOD come from? Why do egregious things happen to good people? Why do I feel more significant than my little body?" I sat up and looked at my hand as if it had never been attached to my body! I yelled out to the Lord, "Why am I here!"

My voice was so loud that the words bounced off the walls so fast and I almost felt my words' commanding presence. The words flew past my head, knocking me out. I laid down flat on my back, my arms and legs stretched wide. Those words took a lot out of me. I began to feel stirred up. I felt those knots in my stomach slowly creeping in the day my mom, sisters, and brother left. Empty and defibrillating shocks went through my body to keep my blood pumping. The tears didn't drip; they poured out as if it was built up for years. I knew the only thing that would soothe my soul was a little fresh air and getting on my knees and pray. I walked over to the window, lifted it halfway, stood there to catch a breeze for a few seconds, and walked over to the end of my bed, dragging my feet like I lost my best friend, even though I had.

Dear Jesus, I want to say I love you and my family too. Oh Lord, please help me. Can you take care of them while they are gone? I am willing not to be selfish this time (tears falling) and ask for them back. Before I could say in Jesus's name, I heard a whisper, a sound that was so crisp and crystal clear. It was blowing through my window with a breath of fresh air and my human instinct was to turn and see where the crisp breeze was coming from. I wanted to convince myself I was not crazy, but I couldn't. My body surely felt planted. The whispers would say… ***Do not cry; I am always with you! Beloved, you have all the tools and gifts you need. Listen to your inner self.***

I was more than comforted by the words; I wished it wouldn't end. I swiftly heard a door slam so hard, shutting my window. There were mumbling, as things fell and shuffled around. I might have been scared, but these familiar sounds awoke me every night. It was my Poppa. He had been drinking a lot more these days and would come home unable to walk upright. Some nights, he would bring women home. He would wake me up from sleep so they could see how cute I was. Hell, if he felt terrific, he'd play his records and make me sing and dance with them all night long. I wasn't too fond of it. On nights like this, Poppa would come home alone and stumble through the house. He would fall over things until his drunken but still piercing voice calls me. His voice would navigate through the house until it found me and set me straight up in my bed. I was gasping for air, forcing me out of dreamland and jumping out of bed.

After that, I cut on every light in the house and cleaned up the major mess that trailed behind him. Poppa was scary; he would blurt out horrible things. I didn't understand his drinking habit, and it was terrible watching him throw up. The stench of drunken blood and death curdled my stomach. To this day, I'm still haunted by the thoughts of an alcoholic locus that would come during nightfall and take over his near-death host. I couldn't do anything right. The more he yelled at me, the more I aimed to please him. I was starting to be terrified of this man. Deep down, I knew he loved me and would never intentionally hurt me. However, his words told a different story. As a child, you're unaware that you are verbally being eradicated. All I knew was that, at this point, the smell of my dad's cologne was enough to petrify me. I began to have the shakes and would cry when I heard loud noises.

House rule number 2256, "Do not speak about what goes on in our house. Don't even speak, for that matter." Since the heavy drinking, every day has grown colder! These events could carry on until about 3 or 4 am. He would fall asleep anywhere in the house but in his bed. The aggressive odor of over-intoxication and cigar smoke filled the house. The perturbation was extremely bad. I always tried being careful so I wouldn't make a sound. More so, the house was old and majority of the house had hardwood floors; let people know someone was up walking around. The squeaky floor didn't help me get back to my room quietly. I never got back in bed without sending up a prayer to GOD. I knew He was busy counseling many prayers and lives, which forced me to make a quick reminder, such as calling a close friend but getting no answer. So you wait a while and call again, but this time you leave a detailed message!

Morning finally came. Poppa would wake me at about 5:50 am sharp. "Up and at them rise and shine, Pugga! Poppa must get to work! You, my dear, have school today." I always woke up abruptly and thanked GOD for waking me up. No good morning Poppa or anything else. Rodell is Poppa's first name. He is from a small town in Arkansas. He grew up knowing ***God the Father, His son, Jesus, and the Holy Spirit,*** and that no man shall enter ***GOD's*** kingdom without confessing ***Jesus*** is ***Lord*** of ***Lords***; He is the ruler of the earth. No matter what, my parents trained me to know the

Lord as best as possible. There were no hard feelings when it came to giving ***GOD's*** first fruits!

Even though I was a child, I knew that if I couldn't say anything nice, then I don't have to say anything. Poppa kept trying to get my attention, but I would ignore his comments and begin with my praises to GOD. Only then did I realize this substance he was consuming at a tremendous rate does make him forget, or maybe he was too ashamed to mention anything because he was back to being Rodell. As endearing as a man of his caliber could be, I was still scared. Trimmers took over my body. On top of it all, I hated going to school. The kids made fun of me; I was a kinky head, little hobo girl with a daddy for a mommy. How embarrassing! The kids didn't let me forget that. I sure didn't let them forget because everytime someone said something, I made sure to kick their ass. I went to school with many kids who had a two-parent home. So, I didn't expect them to understand. I also didn't know why I was suddenly wetting myself; some days three or four times. Peeing on myself was ***normal dysfunction*** for the next couple of years. Some odd years had the nerve to sneak up on me.

However, nothing changed. I wrote Paige almost every day with no return mail, and this was just another reason my heart grew colder. I was ten years old but still having bed-wetting issues. At the time, Poppa was still working, dating, and drinking. As for me, I was still that jumpy, scary, conflicted little girl. Poppa can't seem to figure out why I was always acting strange. How could I tell him I was afraid of so many things? I wasn't given opportunities to express myself, so I stayed mute. When answering questions, whatever did manage to come out was a whisper. People would have to put their ears to my lips to hear me; about time they could figure out one word, they had given up.

It's the summer of the third grade going into fourth, and I was glad to be out for the summer since I loved learning. I just developed a dislike for people. I was fighting every day. Girls, boys, fuck it! Even the teachers and principals could get it. However, I stayed with good grades.

THORN TWO

During the summer, I lived with Aunt Sugar. I was less timid, and I loved it. I was nothing but a little kid at her house. If I had an accident, Nana was as sweet as pie, and she never made me feel wrong about my issues. She would hum her melodies. To my ears, they were like ancient African folktale and very calming. She would talk to me and tell me she loved me and that I was an intelligent, wonderful girl. I wanted to believe her, but how could she be the only one who saw this? This day felt as though I had already been through it before. I stood in Nana's window in just a slight daze. Reality only brought me back when I saw Nana outside in her day gown pacing back and forth. It looked like she was waiting for something or someone. The mailman pulled up and they both talked for a couple of minutes. Then he handed Nanna a stack of mail.

I vividly remember the whole event. This happened a few years back. At that moment, it didn't mean anything but added to the other unusual things that happened to plant themselves in my world. Nana waived bye and looked at all the mail in disbelief. "Is it anything for me?" I asked Nana, as we stood outside. I began to ration with myself. I quickly realized after two and half years I wouldn't get anything. "Nooooo!" Nana said in a loud voice, as snatched away from me in a hurry to get upstairs!

I stopped and stood still for a second, trying to figure out why she raised her voice in such a painful tone. When I decided to let it go, I ran into the house and caught the end of Nana leaving the attic without the stack of mail. A part of me felt like she was hiding something from me. How could she conceal my mom's letters from me? I said to myself, "I'll get them! One way or another." I ran out of the house as fast as possible with no destination in mind, tears filling my eyes. I couldn't see anything but I didn't give a fuck. I was hoping I would run into something or get hit by a car and end up in the hospital. It sounds crazy, but that was my reality. As I was running, I noticed my bottom half was wet again. Fuck this shit! I yelled because I was confused about why this was happening to me. "I really can't control this," I said to myself.

I stopped to wipe my eyes. I looked around, and I was at the park. I went up the hill to sit down in the bushes, not knowing my cousin was in the park with her boyfriend. As I sat down there, she came to me. Her name was Sheila. She stood just as tall as I could remember my brother, Ivonne, to be. She was six feet, very light skin, beautiful curly hair, and had the most prominent mole on her cheek, which acted as a piece of art. She also had Asian-style eyes with a very comforting voice. She and Nana were my favorites. She always took me out alone without the other kids that stayed at Nana's with her kids.

Sheila sat down next to me. She just hugged me, cried with me, and told me that I always made her cry whenever I cry. This made me feel secure about my cousin. Sheila and her man friend took me to the mall and bought me a new outfit and underclothes. I didn't need to contemplate why she did it; she couldn't help but smell and see the urine. Nana didn't want her to make it evident that the other kids were upset, but Sheila didn't care; I was her favorite, and she was mine.

I could smell something so familiar in the air, like Old Spice, Brute, beer, and outdoors. I was so alarmed that I blurted out, "Oh my fucking gosh. Poppa's off already?" I looked around to make sure nobody heard me. The coast was clear. I ran and hid from him for so long and the whole house kept looking for me. I looked straight ahead and saw a pair of feet with steel-toe boots. It was Poppa! Immediately, I grew in fear. "The only place we didn't look is under this table," he said. Suddenly, the tablecloth came up and I was exposed. There was no reason for me to be scared at this point.

Poppa wasn't drunk, although he did smell like he had a couple. On the flip side, tell that to my mind and body. "Come from under there," Poppa said! "Yes, sir," sadly, I replied. Everyone stood around and watched like this was a suspenseful movie, and I was the star. Poppa turned around to acknowledge that we had an audience "You and I have a dinner date!" I want you to meet someone. "I don't want to," I whispered... as if someone could hear me! I slowly crawled out and stood all of four feet. "Well," Poppa said, "no need to get dressed. Where did you get those clothes?"... Before I could say anything, Sheila quickly stood up. In a hurry, she answered, "Uhhh...I bought them." They all knew Poppa didn't like no handouts. He always said we're not poor, and that we are just fine with the help of the Lord! "Oh, okay! Well, thanks, cuz," Poppa said with all excitement. "I like it. Her hair is beautiful as well." Sheila braided my hair into single extensions.

Two hours have passed, and Poppa was all cleaned up and shaved. "Ready?" Poppa asked in a whisper. A "yes" came out with frosty cold air. However, Poppa learned to read my lips so he could avoid stooping over to listen to me. "Well, let's go then!" He stated with eagerness in his voice. I wouldn't dare get excited! I knew he was trying hard to fix us up with a new mommy. Deep down, I wanted Paige. It was embedded in my mind that she didn't want me. I just followed suit on the way to this place. Poppa went over things I needed to remember so I wouldn't put us to shame. It was a long ass list of stupid shit to remember.

I picked the most important and rolled with it. I was accustomed to being a chameleon. I was adapting and being comfortable pretending and fabricating stories; I learned from Poppa. It was second nature that I began to believe some of the things being said to these women to make us look better than we are. My little heart was racing, and I didn't want to fuck this up for him. "Calm your ass down!" I chanted to myself over and over as he rang her doorbell I watched how nervous he was constantly fixing his clothes and patting his picked-out afro!

In a few minutes, an ivory color lady opened the door. She was very slender but stunningly beautiful nonetheless. She had dreamy green eyes with long electrifying lashes. I gave her a quick scan from the crown of her head to her shoes. This lady's attire screamed quintessential; a white long sleeve blouse with ***black roses*** all over it and a light blue jean skirt with a split down the middle stopped at her ankle. Dressy, bedazzled tennis shoes dressed her mid-sized feet. She even had matching rose earrings, necklaces, bracelets, and anklets. Her scent was that of fresh rose petals bow tied with deceit.

Now that I'm aware of this deceitful stench, I had forgotten how beautiful and well-dressed she was! I noticed the black bow tie of smoky darkness reach out and shake my hand. I was standing there in complete bewilderment! As the two adults engaged in a stupid-looking stare-down, I couldn't believe they didn't see what I saw. When this "bow tie" let go of my hand, it caressed my face, smacked me, and then resumed its position. The grown-ups walked into the house as if I wasn't there. My mind was stuck on repeat of the current event that had just happened. Trying to set my thoughts on moving my feet one step at a time has failed me. Poppa grabbed my arm to escort me in the proper direction. We were seated at a long rectangular table that would contain eight persons. "My name is Diamond!" the once nameless lady responded. She headed to the kitchen to grab our food. All I knew was that it smelled yummy! There were three big bowls with plaits underneath. She scooped up some kind of soup out of a big tall pot and put it in the bowls. As I was watching her, I saw a black circle appear around her head.

Uuuuhhhhhhh! I quickly inhaled why gasping for air. I had to keep it to myself, or else I'd be in trouble for messing this up. I looked over to see what she was putting in one of the bowls. It was a dropper full of a bright purple substance. I also noticed she didn't put any in the other two bowls. Anxiety set in, and I didn't know what it was. But more so, who was she giving it to? She put her "witches brew" in front of my dad and everything appeared to be moving very slowly. Diamond looked at me crookedly as she put my dad's bowl down. Before I could blink, I saw her eyes shapeshift. I vividly remember it was black in color. They were diamond-shaped. I almost shit my pants. We haven't even been there for an hour.

However, it felt like father "Time" had slowed down the clock. Diamond joined us at the table and they immediately engaged in eye contact. Something weird was happening! Poppa is drooling immensely! His eyes looked bugged out of his head. I pretended to drop my spoon. They swiftly snap out of it. My food in front of me grew cold as I watched Poppa and Diamond enjoyed each other. The room was filled with laughter. Laughing makes me feel comfortable, and a part of the conversation as well. After all, laughing is contagious! I joined in the laughter, not fully knowing what the matter was all about! It didn't matter. I'm now a part of what once was an intimate one-on-one conversation. Before I knew it, time had sped up and it was about time to say goodbye. One thing I've learned about Poppa is that he usually falls in lust quickly when it came to dating. Diamond would be NO different! Diamond looked like she was half Poppa's age. Sometimes I watched him get dressed and paid close attention to how happy he appeared to be—spinning in the mirror and singing HEY THERE, LONELY GIRL by THE DELFONICS! I chuckled to myself almost too loud, and I had to hurry and cover my mouth! After two dates that didn't include me, I knew where this was headed. Sure enough, Poppa came home one night saying we were moving to our new home. I was a little nervous. I didn't forget how she got all weird towards me at her house. I'll give it a try. After all, I was just a child. WHAT THE FUCK DO I KNOW?

The day we moved in, Diamond was so happy to have a little girl with whom she could go shopping, comb my hair, and buy ice cream cones. All that lasted for one month (in my head, that's what it felt like). On this particular day, Poppa had a contracted construction job requiring him to drive out of town. He would be absent for seven days. Diamond was eager to help Poppa with me! She shouted, "ME…ME…ME!" while raising her hand like a little school kid. I became saturated with a dark feeling. I was not feeling well at all! I turned and looked at Poppa, and said, "But why can't I go to Sugar's?" "NO!" he yelled. "That is out of the way. I would have to go backward to drop you off. You'll stay here with Diamond. She'll get you to school." Judging by Poppa's tone, I knew the conversation was over. Despair took over. "Yes Sir!" I said. With certainty in his voice, he said "NOW... I'LL BE LEAVING IN THE MORNING!" Diamond must have noticed how pale I looked. "Come on, DeMarie, we are going to have fun. You won't miss him much," said the young whore dating Poppa! Then I excused myself to the bathroom. I climbed up on the toilet to get to the sink. There's something about running water that always seemed to soothe me. I had to pull myself together and I knew he would soon follow. Sure enough, I heard a bang on the door. "Are you okay in there?" Poppa yelled. "Come on out!" I wanted to live in the bathroom and never come out. Even at 10, I knew that wasn't reality. I stood tall, put my shoulders back, and took a deep breath. I bowed my head and made a cross from my crown to heart, shoulder to shoulder. I stepped out with more conviction than I had BEFORE I went into the bathroom broken-spirited. It was getting late, and Poppa and Diamond had gone to bed. I slept on the couch. I vividly remember not being able to go to sleep. So, I laid there singing songs. The song that tugged at my heart was, SOMETIMES I FEEL LIKE A MOTHERLESS CHILD by ODETTA. See, Aunty Sugar taught us songs, and this was one of many. I began to sing from the beginning.

My thoughts of Paige started to become vague! All I could do at this point was wonder what she was doing at that moment and if I ever crossed her mind. The tears began to fall. The only thought that plagued my mind was that I may never see her again. I fell asleep with my tears soaking the pillow. A sweet forehead kiss later awakened me from Poppa. He was ready to head out for work. I said bye, followed by I love you, as he closed and locked the door behind him. Trepidation soon blanketed me. I laid on my back, breathing in the energy of peace and exhaling all things bad. In those few minutes, my true self began disconnecting from my flesh! I wasn't scared at all. I felt like I had been there before! My true self hovered over my body. I was in a familiar space. I took the time to be present. I *consciously* didn't know to be "aware"; I just knew and it didn't last long. A peal of horrifying laughter filled the air. What was once two (body and soul) quickly became one again. My eyes opened in awareness! Looking around to find the direction of this sinister sniggering, I was summoned to follow the sound. It was Diamond. She was on the telephone. Rubbing my eyes, I couldn't believe it was her as I had never seen her in this state before. She always went to bed fully clothed, full makeup and hair done. Her blotchy skin stands out first, followed by her raccoon eyes. Her hair was also in big rollers. A bright red sports bra covered her top half with matching red and black spandex. She had on a black peep toe mid-heel shoes with a pom pom on each shoe. Her attire left me in shock. What was even more shocking was her conversation. "Girrrrllll, I'm only wit him cause he be doin that house buildin shiiit!" Then she puffed a long cigarette and continued, "His old ass, does wat eva I need...aahaaaa haaa aaahhh ha ha! I just wanna get rid of da gurl! Like where ha muva at? I am to fine to be some body muva... Oookay! Okay, biiitch, let me call you later. This little orphan, Annie, is about to get my house back clean, after her nasty daddy. Biiiitch, I told you if that foo fuckin around, I will make him regret it!" Diamond slams the phone down. I ran as fast as I could back to the couch before she caught me. My heart was pumping while pulling the blanket over my head. I calm down my breathing, focusing on if I can see her approaching. Then I moved so swiftly. Diamond made no footsteps, instead she hovered over my body.

"WWwwAAAAKKKKKKEEEEEE!!!!!!.....UUUUUUUPPPPPPPP!" as she stood over me.

Diamond snatched the blanket off me. "Do you know how to clean?" she yelled at me. "Yeah!" "Well, get the fuck up and get mah shit clean, den Lil biiiitch." She grabbed me by my ponytail and slung me to the floor. She dragged me from the living room down the hallway to the bathroom, put my face in the toilet and said, "NAH, THERE! START HERE!" "HELL, I AINT CLEANIN SHIT AFTER NO MAN IF I AIN'T GOT TO!" She then shuffled away as I was on my hands and knees. I wasn't going to let anyone see me cry! Although my heart hurts, it was at that moment that it started to grow cold! After a while, Diamond came to get me. She was yelling about having company tonight and needing the whole house cleaned. I didn't know what to expect at this point, so I dared not say a mumbling word. She gave me an old rag and stool, and until 2 pm that day, I was still cleaning. I have had nothing to drink or eat all day. "Dia--mond! Dia--mond!" I screamed until she came. She stood there and looked at me until I spoke. "I'm hungry and thirsty. Can I eat, please?" I pleaded with every fiber of my little being. "EAT? Why should I let you eat?" she replied. I couldn't wrap my mind around who this chick was. Poppa (Rodell) would never believe me. I must have been in deep thought for too long, and would soon be brought back to physical existence from an open-handed slap to the side of my face. I honestly think I saw stars! Suddenly, I felt a loud ringing in my left ear; my ear and nose began to leak. She just stood there looking at me most menacingly. I turned my back quickly to clean myself up. The ringing continued, and my vision became hazy. I was now beginning to feel ill. I just wanted to die; I didn't know precisely what it means to die at ten. However, I DID know that one would no longer be tangible. Before I could go any deeper in thought, I heard a man's voice. I quickly understood that it WASN'T Poppa's voice. The man was shouting, so I couldn't make out the conversation. Everything was muffled. Plus, I was too scared to figure out what was going on as I paced the bathroom floor, wondering if she would remember I was still there. The only thing I knew to do was pray. Nana (Aunty Sugar) taught us how to pray and talk to ***GOD***. With a couple of deep inhales and an even deeper exhale, I somehow channeled the energy and quiet space needed to summon ***GOD***.

"***GOD***, it's me again! I need help down here. Poppa left me with this crazy lady. I'm sooooo scared! Now she is arguing with some man who sounds scary as fuck! ***Lord***, I don't want to be here anymore. I want Poppa. If you help me, I won't ask for anything more. I swear." I realized I said this a lot, but I mean it. "Oh, and can you heal my ear?" Then I did head to chest, shoulder to shoulder before I stood up. I now had the courage of a lion and it was pin-dropping quiet in here. A cold breeze was flowing at a fast speed and the door has been kicked off the hinge.

I saw Diamond sitting on the floor, crying. She picked her head up quickly as she felt my presence. Shivering uncontrollably, she grabbed a couch pillow to cover her bruised-up body and torn sports bra. Her legs were quivering and confused like a baby calf trying to stand straight. She reached to me as though she wanted to pick up a baby, and I moved judiciously toward her. My hands were in a locked state in front of my face. "Please forgive me," I said in a voice that didn't sound sincere. She would chant this at least fifty times, possibly to believe in herself. All I could think about was she was lying and I told myself, "DeMarie, don't believe her." She walked me to the kitchen, and had me sit at the table to fix me something to eat. "Wait here," she stated. "I need to call someone to fix my door!" I sat at the table long enough for her to be out of sight. After the morning and evening, I had no appetite any longer. After getting her door fixed, she was reticent with me. She spent most of her time on the phone. I wondered if Rodell called to check in with us. Hell, if he did at this point, I'm sure she wouldn't tell me. She continued to be mean to me for the next few days. Little shit like bumping up against me, sticking her foot out to trip me and pull my hair, make me clean her walls, and wash her clothes. She wouldn't say much anymore, but she made her demands clear. The day before Rodell was due to come back, Diamond got a call from a friend saying they saw him with another woman. That sent Diamond on a rampage! She was speaking in words I didn't understand. Whatever this hoe was saying wasn't English to me! Later in life, I would find out she was speaking creole. She was playing music that sounded backward! She was burning some sticks. That shit smelt nasty! This girl is crazy. I wanted away from her. ***JESUS, WHERE ARE YOU?*** While Diamond was doing whatever she was doing in that room, it felt HEAVY! I couldn't make out everything she was doing. I could see that she wasn't herself, or was she? She must have felt my presence because she lifted her nose to sniff the air. She got up and stomped to the door while running. She opened her door and handled me like a rag doll. In a deep unfamiliar voice, she looked me squarely in the face. With her shapeshifting eyes, she said, "YOU GOTTA GOOOOOOOOO! PACK YALL SHIT." She spun me around and pushed me down on the floor. I was pissed! I screamed at her, with my face still in the carpet. "I FUCK--ING HAAAAAATE YOOOOOUUUUUU!!! I HOPE U DIIIIIIIIIIIIIIIIIE!!!!" I knew this would cost me, but I didn't care. I had it with this cunt. She snatched me up by my clothes so fast. Diamond slammed me against the wall by my throat with a death grip. I surely thought I was going to get my wish; to meet my maker, maybe. No tears, no struggling ssshhhiiiiiid! I was ready. At this point, I must have deserved all I was getting. I was willing to accept my fate. I must have blacked out. I woke up with my hands moving in a 3D fashion and saw stars floating around too. I saw Diamond scampering around the house with a bag and clothes, dropping stuff along the way. I did not even care to pick that stuff up. I watched in confusion. She grabbed her keys and took the stuff to her car, and was talking to herself.

She was cursing and much more. Lastly, she grabbed my arm, hurrying me along. Quicker than my legs could move, I stumbled and tripped over my feet as she dragged me. We got to her car and drove away. I watched the trees as we passed and would count them. Anything to get my mind off the uncertainty of what would happen to me. I wiped away the one tear that snuck out with my shirt. I didn't want her to see me crying. She slammed on the brakes.

Sending me flying to the front of the car, she got out, opened her trunk, and started to throw our belongings all in the street. She put two duffle bags at a bus stop and walked over to the car yelling. Then she said, "Get the fuck out of my car, you little bitch. Go over there, sit at that bus stop and wait for you punk ass daddy here." She then handed me an envelope with two dollars and fifty cents in change. She got in her car and sped off so fast that she almost hit someone. It took me a helluva long time to figure out that no one was coming to save me. I felt completely safe enough to let out a wallow of pain! If ever there was a war cry from a child, that was my reality. It was starting to get dark and realized I must make a move. "Find a store!" a quiet voice said to me.

I looked around to see who it was, but no one was there! I grabbed hold of my two bags that were too heavy to carry; I don't know how the strength in me came about. I had just enough to drag those bags to the nearest store in what felt like miles away. I finally made it to the store. I go to the cooler and got a can of 7up and a bag of Cheetos. Back in the day, it wasn't uncommon for little kids to come to the store alone. I only stood out because of the bags I was dragging, as well as how broken and bruised I appeared. I got to the counter and paid for my stuff. I asked for the nearest pay phone, as I fought back my hurt and tears. Aunty Sugar taught us so much. As an adult today, I never thought I needed her survival skills and life lessons so early on. With that being said, all the kids knew her phone number by heart. I dragged my bags to the pay phone and used my bags as support to stand. I almost fell dialing Nana's number as fast as I could. I was certain someone would answer. At Nana's, someone was always there to answer the phone. I didn't have any luck the first time, so I tried again but there was no answer. I became scared even more. Fuuuuck, can my luck get any worse? Luckily, Nana answered. Nana, it's Pugg! I cried so much that I couldn't get much out to tell her all that had happened. "Pugg honey, I can't hear you! Where are you?" I couldn't even tell here exactly. But I knew I was at a store by Diamond house. She had me get the address of the building. At the time, we also didn't have GPS, so one had to know their city and count blocks. "Go inside the store and tell the store clerk what is happening. I'll send Uncle JOE! The wait was one I'll never forget. All I had was time to think of going back to Sugar's house.

Even though I felt my ***second thorn*** growing, all praises to Jesus were due for answering my prayer to get the hell out of there. My ***hope*** was restored.

HOPE

A feeling of expectation and wish for a sure thing to happen.

My definition of Hope

Is to wish for positive results in any given situation.

3 Keys to Improving your Hope

1. Celebrate your Milestones. Treating yourself to something special. Pat yourself on the back. Acknowledge that things won't always work out as planned, and it is okay.
2. Take time to be inspired. Find circles of people who are where you want to be. Listen to inspirational music and movies.
3. Get Involved. Volunteer your time. Spreading cheer and Hope will cultivate more of it in your surroundings.

THORN THREE

Falling asleep in the car, we were at Sugar's when I woke up. Uncle Joe walked me to the door and told me to go inside, highlighting that he would see me in the morning. As obedient as I was, I nodded my head and proceeded through the door. I was looking for Aunt Sugar and I called out her name…but no answer. I roamed around the house to look for her and couldn't find her anywhere. As I approached the bottom of the long dark stairs, the last place to look was the attic. I heard something, and it sounded like a mail was being opened. I quietly but swiftly moved up the stairs. As I got to the top of the stairs, there was Sugar. With the letters that I've been sending to mommy Paige!!! Could it BE?!

She'd been deceitful to me this whole time. Could it be that the one person I thought would NEVER deceive, hurt, or harm me was doing just that???? In that moment of truth, I vowed to myself, so help me GOD. I WILL NOT EVER IN LIFE TRUST A SOUL!!!! I stood there in a daze, soaking and sobbing. I felt my entire being melting to the floor after losing minutes. I pulled myself together and hurried down the stairs. I thought to myself, what a horrible person in the past I must have been to mirror the things life has thrown at me at such a young age. I cried myself to sleep.

As time passed, many exciting things and some not-so-great things happened. I overcame obstacles despite the odds. At this point in my story, I was about age eleven. I was becoming more aware of myself, my abilities, and my spiritual awakeness. At this time in my life, I knew there was some connection between me and the MOST HIGH *GOD.* One day, I was talking to GOD and asking Him to clarify what I BELIEVE TO BE, which was something FALLACIOUS within me!! I found a book on spiritual prophecy. I began thumbing through the book and piecing together the words I could make out. It was apparent that I had similar things happening to me. Looking at people with my natural eye that others can't see, I felt divine energy around me and in others. I could feel the presence of something sinister too, as I would constantly think and speak words that manifest right before my eyes. Let us not forget my visions. If prophecy were your calling, a high prophet from the church would point it out. Back then, telling people about these things wasn't "***OF GOD***," especially as there weren't a lot of resources, just the library. To me, I assumed that I was BAD, wicked, and destined to dance with the chief evil spirit. I thought GOD needed to deliver me from evil. Later, I discovered the negative things given to me by what felt like a syringe. It flowed through my veins and found its way roaming through the halls of my mind (house of consciousness) to the door that read Belief System (subconscious). The foul words would soon feed off the Core Beliefs in my subconscious.

The visions became stronger, and the eyes became more conditioned to see 4D and beyond. I started to dream more, sleep, and stay awake. I began to feel more energy as my abilities grew. I can remember playing outside, and my dad was outside washing his orange truck. It was a Dotson flatbed with a canopy top. I can remember this day as clear as the sea. One of my favorite things to do as a child was jump rope. While I was outside jumping, I could see my reflection on the orange truck. As I watched myself jump up and down, I got another dreamy tunnel-like vision. Poppa and I are driving in this orange truck, and it appeared we were going somewhere. We reached this destination and pulled up to a massive home. This home stood on a high hill overlooking the city. Poppa got out and left me in the truck, and the truck began to roll down a hill. Just like that, the vision was over. Once things were back to looking familiar around me, I was in my comfort zone. I felt soooo relieved. I can't lie, I was a little shaken; an engulfed feeling wanted to get me down. Yet and still, nothing was going to get in the way of practicing for JUMP ROPE FOR HEART. I threw that vision in one of the closets in my mind that read mind movies and continued to jump rope. A few weeks passed, Poppa and I got our routine morning started. We headed out of the house and got to the truck. I extended my hand to the door handle and seized my hand back as quickly as I could. I wasn't expecting to "see" anything. Well, I did; it was the big house that sat on the hill I had seen weeks before. Poppa opened the door for me. It was a quiet drive. "Pugg, I need to stop by a friend's house before I take you to school, okay?" My throat suddenly became desiccated. A very dry "yes" came out. He pulled up and told me to wait in the car as he ran upstairs. I patiently waited as I sat in the car. The longer it took him, the more I grew worried. I began to wonder why he was taking so long. It felt like an hour had passed, as I waited for him to turn up. It was a school morning and I was in my uniform, wondering if I would be late for school. I was also hoping not to miss out on breakfast. We had my favorite; pancake on a stick!!! SUDDENLY, the truck started moving in slow motion. I looked out the window and found that the truck was moving. As the truck moved, I noticed the clouds passing swiftly and the trees were waving. The truck was facing down the hill at the time Poppa got out. It picked up momentum. This old, heavy-weight work truck began to roll swiftly, effortlessly down a steep hill. Sitting up in a hurry, I realized this wasn't supposed to happen, but it was. FIGHT OR FLIGHT kicked in, as I remembered the vision I had a few weeks ago. As this happened, my body's nervous system turned on due to the hormones released. When you are in a scary situation, your heartbeat speeds up, your breathing becomes rapid, and your body is tense and ready to take action. The ACTION would be to FIGHT or RUN (FLIGHT). I was struggling to take off my seatbelt, so I could unlock the door and get out. Jiggling the belt back and forth and squeezing the button was the hardest thing to do. While trying to look out the window, I began screaming hysterically for someone to help me. Heeeelp!!!!!!! PLEEEEEEAAASE!!!!! HEEEELP!!! POPAAAAA!!! POPPPPAAAA!!! At that moment, I felt that Jesus was ALL I had to call on. I screamed for Jesus to save me and not let me die. GOD, where are you? The bellow of energy I had no longer existed. I continued to scream DADDY (I hardly ever called him dad or daddy). In distress, the order went out the window. Once I got the seat belt off, I got up to see what was happening around me. The truck was screeching and screaming for help, just like I was. I opened my eyes wide as the truck headed for a cliff at that very moment. I reached for the lock on the door and pulled it up to release the door. The mutherfucking lock won't budge! Climbing to the driver's side, I forgot that the plastic cover on the lock was missing; you can only open it with pliers. Poppa took the pliers with him, and I cried even more. Turning the steering wheel wasn't working either. For some reason, it was hard for me. I thought of everything; feelings of being defeated, lonely, scared, and afraid. My vision became blurry. I scanned the truck one more time, but this time I looked all around. Then I saw a small window that connected the canopy in the back of the truck, and I knew I could get back there. I've climbed through it before so I knew I could get it done. I built up the fight so I could take flight! Soon as I stood, the truck took a plummet down the cliff. I closed my eyes, knowing this was IT for me at eleven. The ultimate cause of death was thinking I was a bad girl. I was doing bad things in my heart, so I didn't deserve to live. I was certain GOD was pissed the fuck off with me. After all, I did many things I shouldn't have done. For example, I would steal Poppa's cigarettes he would leave in the ashtray, or cussing. Yeah, that's it. I did a helluva lot of that. I also thought about Paige and my brother and sisters. I didn't know what to do. I've run out of life at this point. The truck slammed into what

I thought was the ground. I hadn't opened my eyes yet for fear of the unknown. Have I crossed over? Will I now have my dance with evil? I believed I was as good as dead. Immediately I opened my eyes, the view scared me to tears again. I could see the dirt piles down below and a bunch of junk trash that was sure to catch fire if the truck fell. I hurried to the back window, making the truck rock. Fuck! I couldn't get to it, for gravity was pulling me downward. I looked out the window as I heard Rodell's voice screaming, saying that he was sorry and would get me out of there. Within seconds, the police, ambulance, fire truck, tow truck, and anything you could think of were at my rescue. I thanked GOD for keeping me safe. In that very second, my life could have been over. I thanked GOD. I thanked Jesus!! I stored this experience in the room of my mind that read Core Beliefs. I knew GOD would be there for me, but once again, would MAN? ANOTHER ***RED THORN*** GREW INSIDE ME!

Rodell continued to be a serial dater. This time, he didn't allow them to meet me unless he saw them fit as a real candidate to help him raise me and be a family.

Rodell had realistic goals in life. He was nothing different than any other God-fearing man. He wanted "a normal life" so bad for me, and I believe he lost himself in the process. Rodell began to drink more and more; he never really drinks hard liquor, mostly beer. He would kill a twenty-four pack in one night; he was a functioning addict. In one of our father and child moments, Rodell told me that he started working at the age of six. It was definitely in him to be a working man. Once he started drinking, he would keep calling me out of my room to throw away his empty can and bring him a new one. That was when I began to count the cans. Of course, I didn't understand what beer was exactly. I knew I wasn't allowed to drink, and Poppa now seemed different. Stumbling, not making sense with his words, and also yelling, he would say i*t's my fault he wasn't happy* while crying. He also said *no man would love me because I bring negative things around.* The worst experience I had at this age was throwing up blood; lots of blood every night. Yet, I would stay up all night, making sure he was okay. I believe if I did everything he needed without asking, I could change his mind about me. In his sleep, he would choke. Holding his head in my lap at eleven was traumatizing. I just knew one day I wouldn't be able to help him. Washing and throwing away bloody clothes, some days I would go to school with blood underneath my fingernails. I would try to take a shower and scrub, but the fucking shit wouldn't go away. I would always fall asleep in class, get into fights, and get bullied. Hey, I was a fucking kid in pain every day of my life. Nobody truly noticed. But being a bad kid was the only thing that didn't go unnoticed. Not even the fact that at eleven, I have uncontrollable wetting during the day. How was I supposed to know what I needed, or why I was wetting myself? The Core Belief (subconscious) room was starting to overflow with false words and bad memories. At eleven, I couldn't figure out where to store my experiences. I now believe that our body sets off an alarm that is recognized as anxiety, depression, and out-of-control sensory; it tells us we are putting stuff in the wrong rooms or that you are creating new rooms to STUFF. I call these feelings ***Thorns.*** Between the time Paige disappeared and up into my now eleven-year-old self, I had encountered quite a few people in my life who never had my best interests at heart. I was never accepted by most and misunderstood. I didn't have the teachings that a little girl should have. It wasn't all Poppa's fault; he was a male. It wasn't all bad with Poppa. We did fun stuff and would play with me and bought me cool things. He would share things with me from his childhood, both good and bad. He was smart too! He was also a natural artist who would graduate from the ART INSTITUTE of Seattle, Washington. I remember going with him some days because he didn't have a sitter, and would beg his teachers to let me stay that I was a good kid and would be quiet. They always let me stay because I was good and cute. My childhood was 80/20. 80% bad in my eyes and 20% good. When it was good, it was GOOD. When it was bad, it was BAD. Rodell went on to be in a relationship with a lady named Sandraya. Sandraya was just as toxic at times as Poppa!

She had a drinking problem. She also liked this white substance that looked like baby powder, sugar, or salt. What I now know to be cocaine. She had a five-year old son. His name was Julien. Julien was bad as fuck. He threw tantrums when he couldn't get his way. He was mean to everyone and loved to hit people. I could see why Rodell liked Sandraya.

She was a tall, fair-skinned woman. Back then, one of the terms used to describe someone who had one Caucasian parent and one black parent was mulatto. Mulatto was the term Poppa used to illustrate Sandraya's background. I didn't care as long as she was good to us. I didn't mind her badass son, either. I had a desire (HOPE) for good things to come. Thanks to my truck accident, this time, I knew exactly where to store my emotion. Julien seemed to like me; he did hit me at times or cussed at me, but when he saw that I was just like him, he left me alone. I can honestly say I loved her and she touched my heart. She was the first of the bunch who would attempt to love me back and teach me to sit with my legs closed and not like I was "Al Bundy." I admit I was oblivious to how a little girl was supposed to act. Keeping up the act was hard work. I had to have my hair combed, which was total bullshit. I even had to wear skirts and dresses, socks with ruffles and dumbass shoes with stupid heels on them. Ooooh!!! I was suuuuuch a FUCKING GIRL! So much so that I had my modeling catwalk DOOOWN. Let me tell you a little about when Sandraya was teaching me how to walk. I hiked up my dress with my toes pointed outward, which made me look like I a cowboy who just got off a horse ride. She laughed hysterically. Julien followed suit. It was so catchy; hell, I started to laugh too. I got a glimpse in the mirror, and boy, I did look like a girl raised by a man. I fell on the floor laughing, but right inside of me, I knew it wasn't funny at all. I realized that I WAS different. Sandraya and Julien scooped me up and hugged me so tight. Hugging was something new to me because I didn't know how to feel. Was I supposed to do something too? I yelled in a barbaric way, which was natural to me. They quickly let go and just stared at me. I got up, ran outside and started to cry. What I thought I wanted wasn't IT at ALL. I just wanted Paige. Why can't I be with heeeeer? I didn't care to share my feelings with anyone. I didn't trust a soul, so I always lied about what was ailing me. Sandraya hurried behind me to console whatever I was going through. This time, when she reached out to touch me, I was petrified. I wasn't the same child I was a few mins ago. The tug of war continued. I would carry on acts considered "unnatural" for little girls to do. I had to stay at Sandraya's house one day cause Poppa had one of those construction contracts where he had to travel at least one week at a time. Waking up at 5 am was normal for me. I was on Rodell's schedule. While we are getting ready to go, I would get the usual talk about being good. Blah! Blah! Blah!! The one thing that stood out this time was Poppa saying to me with thunder in his voice, "DON'T LET NOBODY IN YO HEAD. I MEAN THAT SHIT!" He grabbed my face so hard my cheeks began to touch. "LAST TIME I LET A FUNKY BITCH DO YOUR HAIR, IT FELL OUT!" I couldn't speak because he still had my face. Hell, I think he spaced out for a few seconds. I'm sure he was thinking about the event with my hair. I nodded my head since I couldn't say a word. Even if I could, I knew better! I headed straight for the bathroom to brush my teeth. While in the mirror, I realized I needed to shave. I put on some of Poppa's shaving cream and grabbed the nearest razor. Had I shaved before? NO! I had a play set I used for my dolls. Today, I wanted to mimic Poppa. I wanted to know why he was doing it. Ahhh! I could see how satisfying it was to shave. As soon as I took the next stroke. I cut my cheek so deep. I was now leaking like a faucet, screaming and crying. Poppa rushed into the bathroom to see what had just happened. "Girl, what did you do?" He laughed. Guess he never saw a funnier sight at the moment. "I just want to be like yooou," I said. "Listen, Pugg, some things you aren't going to be able to do because you are a girl and Poppa is a man. Do you understand?" "Yeeeaahh!" "Good girl!" he said as he cleaned up the cut on my cheek. He dressed me with a band aid that would cover up my dysfunction. Our bags were packed, and we headed out to Sandraya's house.

Upon arrival, Poppa walked me to the door. He hugged and kissed Sandraya, and thanked her. Poppa told me he loved me, kissed my forehead, and disappeared into the thick Seattle fog. Instantly, I began to feel unwell. Feelings of the past would inundate the void and I began to retch, but I couldn't come up with anything. I wanted to soooo bad. Puking always made the "belly ache" feel better. I sprinted through the house, looking for the bathroom as my bags hit every corner on the way. At that point, I just needed a way out. I closed and locked the door. Sandraya didn't want to bother me cause she didn't come knocking, and I was okay with that. I just wanted to be alone since I only trusted myself. My eyes were getting heavy. I laid down in the tub, using my bag as pillow. After a cat nap, I slowly got up and went straight to the sink. My life felt like a movie. I looked in the mirror to see if it was real, which I did leisurely. Puffy, bloodshot eyes. I squeezed my chubby, high cheekbones. YUP! Sure enough, I was still here. I didn't know HOW I expected it to be IF I was ever to die. I just assumed it was better than what I was feeling. One thing I do know was that I was just a product of two people who once loved each other. I pulled myself together and headed out to find Sandraya. Yelling chatter filled the air. I couldn't quite figure out the words. My left ear and eye hadn't healed yet. The closer I got, the clearer things became. "Please, baby, I need you," said Sandraya. "I, I, I swear I'll pay you back. I can't work unless I'm happy..yah know." There was a long pause on the phone.

Sandraya hung up the phone and it rang again. She picked up quickly. "Look, if you…" said Sandraya before her voice changed to a familiar tone that I recognized. "Hey, how's it going?" she inquisitively asked. "She is fine. She is sleeping in the tub. Have you had any luck finding a place?" asked Sandraya. At that moment, I knew it was Rodell. I moved a little closer, hoping not to make a sound. Was I hearing her clearly? "Well, did you get everything moved out?" she sounded like she had many more questions to ask. She was also trying to be as quiet as possible. "Keep trying. It will work itself out," Sandraya repeated. "My door is always open," she mentioned before saying her salutations. I ran to the living room and sat on the floor. Not long after, Sandraya came looking for me. "Hi, Pugg. How are you? Did you get some rest?" she asked before I could answer the first question. Sandraya continued to ask me distracting questions. As if she knew I was going to ask if she had spoken to Poppa yet, she went straight into the kitchen to fix our brunch. I assumed that Julien only got up because he smelled the sausage and bacon. After having our first meal of the day, Sandraya proceeded to do my hair. I instantly panicked. Everything Poppa said echoed in my ears. "NO...NO..NO..!!!!! I'M GOING TO GET IN TROUBLE!!! PLEEEASE!" I continued to plead with her over and over, hoping she would hear my heart crushing. Not only that, I felt my ass hurting from that whooping I was about to get for letting this heffa on my head. What was she up to? I just couldn't tell. Sandraya washed and braided my hair in two pigtails and one in the back. I swear I cried the whole time she braided it. At first, I couldn't wait to see Poppa, but NOW I didn't care to see him any time soon. After a couple of hours of hair braiding and crying, she was finally done. She quickly rushed Julien and me out to play. My instinct told me she was up to something. I would constantly come back and look in the windows to see if I could find anything. I didn't catch anything unusual, except that Sandraya was getting dressed. Her clothing was concise and revealing; a form-fitting black dress. This dress stopped right under the cusp up her butt cheek. Then she put on the highest heels I've ever seen. Her fair skin tone looked like silk, plus a heavy makeup on her bright red lips. Her flat ironed hair down past her shoulders completed the look she wanted. Sandraya checked her watch for time. Grabbing her purse in a hurry, she headed to find us. "JULIEN!!" "PUGG!!" she screamed through the screen door. "I'LL BE RIGHT BACK! COME INSIDE!! Don't open my door," she said, while closing the door behind her. As soon as she was gone, I said to Julien, "I'll be back. Don't open the door." I quietly hurried behind her. After all the shit I heard today, curiosity set in. I ran and sat on the stairs. The path of the stairs was covered by bushes, so I hid behind them. Sandraya's heels met with the gravel without a pattern to follow. She stopped to light a stick. After she made donuts come from her mouth, I knew she was smoking a cigarette and watched her in admiration. The way she held her smoke in her hand led me to believe she was a consistent smoker. It was starting to get dark and I saw a long black car come around the corner. It had glossy dark windows. I quickly looked at Sandraya wondering. Could this be why she paced back and forth? She smiled with glee. The person pulled right up in front of her. He rolled his window down and motioned for her to get in the back seat. The back door flew open. I could see some dark color street shoes with black pants. My smile was slowly turning upside down! Who the fuck is this guy? I didn't want to think too hard about it. I mean, hell, it could be her Pops for all I knew. But then I asked myself, "Why would she be waiting at night, outside for family?" Sandraya shuffled her feet in her heels. I could hear them loudly tapping against the concrete. Her perturbation quickly turned to elation. She still had her smoke in hand, ashes falling along the way. The window of the car stayed down. The man hands her something and she quickly put it in her bra. Seconds later, the guy put his hand around Sandraya's throat and forced himself on her. Sandraya's head was rested in the window seal and she struggled with the force he was putting on her. I grew more and more concerned by the second. Not fully aware of what was happening, I knew the act was unwanted. I covered my face with my hands as I tried hard to stabilize them, but I still couldn't help but peek. After the guy stopped hurting her, yelled at her by saying some words to her but she didn’t say anything. Before I knew it, the man pushed her out of the car onto the ground. She looked down to acknowledge the blood dripping from her leg. The guy threw her shoes at her, which hit Sandraya on the head. BASSSTAAARD!!!!!!! She screamed as she dragged the word. The man's tires made a loud sound as he drove off!! I was so shocked by what I had just seen. I had the urge to comfort her as she usually did with me, but I remembered I needed to get in the house before she saw me. I ran into the house and turned on the TV. I couldn't figure out if I should lay down and play sleep or if watching TV was good enough. Pretending to be asleep was my best option. I laid on the couch with my eyes closed. Sandraya's ass didn't even fucking notice me. She was zombie-like; slowly walking into the house. I could hear her sniffling and whimpering as she passed me. I could feel something had lowered her frequency. She went into her room and didn't bother closing the door. At this point in my life, I knew I had to watch the adults around me and every action they exhibited. I learned so much just by watching. The tears that ran down her face made her mascara look like coal. I knew that she was not feeling good about the choice she had made. She snapped out of her star gaze to pull the white envelope out of her bra. At that moment, whatever she felt suddenly turned into peer bliss. Following her euphoria, she began to sing, "I'm a little teapot short and stout. Here is my handle. Here is my spout." Reality must have set in because her laughter turned to pain. Even still, she poured the grainy white substance on the dresser and took one card from a deck. She chopped the stuff with a card and grabbed a straw. By this time, I was already drooling. I couldn't even imagine WHAT she was going to do. I noticed her bending down. She closed one nostril, and the shit on the dresser vanished line after line. I stopped counting after four. In between those "lines," she would make sounds that equated to some pain and discomfort. Surely, the stuff that she put in her nose gave her superpowers; she was moving so swiftly. I had a light bulb moment. "Could it be that Sandraya is a superhero mom? Maybe she fights crime. She is so amazing," I started to think to myself. Maybe if I get a chance to talk to her, she can help me find Paige. I got a little excited as I drifted off in thought. Sandraya grabbed all her belongings and left before I could even ask her anything. The door slammed with my hand stuck in mid-air, ready to flag her down like a taxi. My mind quickly told me to follow her. But before then, I went and made sure Julien was good. He was sound asleep. So, that became my pass to leave. I began to panic because I thought I had lost her to the night. As a little girl, there wasn't much I feared. I caught up to Sandraya blocks away from her house. Seeing what this super mom was doing in the night was staggering. After all, this was when an enormous amount of iniquitous acts of evil took place. I took my seat on the stoop of an abandoned house. Overlooked by its odious appearance, I knew nobody would notice me. Uncertain of what was about to take place, I was beginning to fall asleep. I cuffed my chin with my hands and rested them on my knees so that I could stay awake. I wrestled with just going back home. All Sandraya did walking back and forth, flagging down cars. Not sure what she was doing, but it looked like she needed to ask a question or something. I thought to myself, "Would someone answer the lady's question?" I was so happy that someone was about to listen to her question. Suddenly, the man handed her some money she put in her purse and proceeded to unzip his pants. I covered my face quickly and uncovered it. My heart was out of rhythm. I am sweating profusely. The act was over. She jumped out of the car as fast as she could and the man swiftly drove off. Sandraya was back, trying to get someone to notice her. As I took a few moments to assess the scene, I noticed other women were doing the same thing. Why do these ladies come out in the night to ask flipping questions? When I realized that I needed to think like a grown-up and try to figure it out, I had to move closer. But how? I waited until

Sandraya got in her next car. I decided to sit down on the curb. These ladies were too busy even to notice me. As a child, so many things are unclear that you can make crazy assumptions about. You start to look within your mind's hallway to find the right door to store new words or experiences. Even if that meant putting it in the wrong room until another experience happens, that makes it clear to the mind that it belongs in another room.

I was about to learn a valuable lesson about my child-like thinking. The more my curiosity grew, the closer I got. This time, I told myself I was going to sneak in the car. Almost in cinque when Sandraya opened her door, so did I. The conversation went something like this "Hey Jonny, you' looking for a good time?" Jonny stated, "I sure am, momma!" "Good!" Sandraya said with a sinister sound to her voice. "I charge sixty dollars for a blow job…" "A blow job?" My little mind repeated almost so loud that I thought they could hear me. I covered my mouth, hoping my mind wouldn't shout out another word. She continued to tell him, "Full service, one hundred dollars." At this point, I was taking note. Jonny said, "Hell yeah, I want some of your sexy ass." "Well, let's take a ride," Sandraya said with pleasure. The man took off so quickly that his tires were spinning. At this point, I was scared cause I didn't want my cover blown. We didn't get too far, and he parked the car. He leaned his seat back. It was pitch black there. There was a big goose-down winter coat on the floor I had put over me, which almost suffocated me. I needed to know what was going on. The man handed her money and she began to unzip his pants. This time I watched it! OH, MY FUCKING GOSH!!! She was touching his private part. I instantly started sweating again. I wanted to go home. I kept watching as Sandraya was rubbing her hands all over his "private". Jonny then said, "Put it in your mouth and suck it, you dirty bitch." He grabbed her by the back of her neck while pulling her hair. I could tell she was getting pissed. Forcing her mouth on him, she continued with the act. While still holding her by her hair, he asked her to sit on it. Sandraya looked like her soul had left her body, but she did it. Afterward, the man began to breathe heavily, and his body jerked like he was dying. Tears fell from my eyes. I couldn't wrap my mind around what the fuck just happened. The guy snapped out of it, pushed her off him, and pulled out a knife. Putting it up to her throat, she said, "Heeey!! HEY! HEY! MAN?! I THOUGHT WE WERE HAVING A GOOD TIME." Jonny yelled, "SHUT THE FUCK UP, HOE!! GIVE ME MY MONEY BACK, AND I WON'T KILL YOU!" Sandraya reached the floor of the car and grabbed my leg as she observed that someone was in there. She found her purse. Psssssshhhhh! Something was sprayed. The man started choking and coughing. Trying to get to Sandraya, she grabbed his knife and stabbed him repeatedly! I could no longer hold it in. I was about to pass out from all my eyes had seen. My lungs, throat, and eyes filled with this substance she sprayed. Crying and throwing up followed. I was busted, but at this point, I didn't care; I just wanted to get out of there. Sandraya would have continued stabbing the man but shifted her attention to me. "OH, MY FUCKING GOSH!! GIRL, WHAT THE FUCK...HOW THE FUCK DID YOU? NEVERMIND, I'VE GOT NO TIME FOR YOU NOW. GET OUT OF THE CAR AND WAIT FOR ME!" Not able to see, I used my hands as a guide. Sandraya was mumbling and cussing him out for making her do this as she dragged his leaking body to the ground. She kicked him and took his wallet. Then she shoved a clear balloon in his mouth with a white substance in it.

I was trembling uncontrollably that I wet my pants. Sandraya flushed my eyes with a nearby water hose, then yelled, "COME ON PUGG, GET IN THE CAR!" Not much conversation in the car. She rubbed my head. "I'm so sorry you had to see that! With tears in her eyes she said, “I'll explain to you later! Right now, I've gotta get you home so I can dump this car!" I couldn’t even talk. I was withdrawn and shocked. We pull up at her house and she asked me to hop out, and that she would see me when daylight hit. She had to get back to work.

I hugged her, and before I got out of the car, she gave me the guy's knife and told me to put it in her room. Soon as I touched the door knob, my eyes closed. I saw the black car Sandraya got in earlier was parked in her garage. With little energy, I inhaled and opened the door, heading straight for the garage. It felt eerie inside. Sure enough, the car was there. What was he doing here? All the lights were off except the one over the stove and the glow from under Julien's room. I was checking every room before I woke up Julien with my paranoia. This guy wasn't to be found. I was quietly cracking the door open, scanning the room. My breathing got heavier. I heard a smacking sound. My eyes was fixated on a similar act as Sandraya.

When a child is learning about new animals in life, he will associate any animal he has previously known with this new download. For instance, a cheetah might be mistaken for a cat or dog, because they all have familiar body parts. As I have stated many times, until someone comes along and puts a name to the new object word or experience, it will remain in the wrong room of our overworked minds. This gut-wrenching experience now goes in its separate category. The molestation/rape room.

Julien's pants was around his ankles. Hugging the outside of his feet sat a pair of grown man's shoeless feet. I was scared to follow where my eyes wanted to go. I did it anyway. Julien's hands were behind his back, and the man was holding them. The man was making the same noise the guy Sandraya was with when she was sitting on his penis. I really wanted to see Julien's face. I was unhinged. I didn't hear a sound from Julien. Julien's face told a story of its own; one of helplessness and distress. Julien had mentally checked out. I realized he needed help. "How am I going to help him?" Forgetting I had a knife in my hand was the best decision. I believe he would have raped and killed us both. I quietly ran outside grabbed a loose brick from her flower bed, and threw it through the front windshield of his car. Then I hid behind the garage door. I was scared as fuck behind that door! I put my fear aside to save Julien. I activated my FAITH! I had FAITH GOD was going to answer my silent prayer to send Sandraya home soon. Fumbling through the house to get to the garage, I heard the man's voice growing closer. He turned on the light and stood there quietly. My intuition said, "GO!" immediately, I charged at him. "Aaaahhhhhhhhhhhhhhhh!!!!! MOTHERFUCKER!!" I knocked his legs below and a loud thud echoed through the bare walls. The blood gushing from his head indicated he had hit his head. If there was one thing I learned from a scary movie, it is that the bad guy never dies. I looked down at my feet. There spun the knife I was once holding. I picked it up, knowing if I DIDN'T, he would. I found rage in me again when I saw ghostly Julien come behind me. I closed my eyes and charged at this creep. I was stabbing him in his back as he laid face down. A fountain of REDRUM spouted from his back. Closing the door on him and locking it, Julien and I held each other and cried. I decided to put all kinds of stuff up against the door in case he woke up. Julien and I cleaned up and laid on the couch with a kitchen knife in hand until Sandraya got home.

It was morning because the roosters let me know. Soon after I realized Sandraya wasn't there, she entered the door. I stood up so fast that Julien fell to the floor. I started screaming,

"YOUR BOYFRIEND HURT JULIEN!!!" Having to relive this shit gave me heart palpitations. As I was crying, Sandraya yelled, "Julien, what's going on?" "He's been hurting me every time you leave, momma!" "Where is he?" We both pointed to the garage. Like a bat out of hell, she ran to the garage. She removed stacked chairs and a table away before reaching the door. With her mase in hand, she opened the door. She screamed so loud that it scared us. She bent down to check his pulse. Oh my GOD, he is still alive. "Pugg, come here, honey. Tell me what happened?" I rehearsed what had happened with her. "Look AT ME!" she said while shaking me. "We can't tell your dad about any of this, okay? Pinky swear." "I pinky swear!" This would be the first secret I ever had to keep. Even as a child, our life was tested. Unconsciously, we will respond based on the things we store in the subconscious hallway of our minds! In my case, my core belief system started with GOD!

THORN FOUR

My unique life experiences allowed me to activate my FAITH in GOD. I called on Him to act on situations I had no control over. In return, the building blocks of HOPE had created a new room all on its own. Expectation and my unspoken desire was a building block, but they also gave me the master key to the room of HOPE. This room of HOPE was where I will store the word TRUST.

I knew when Rodell called home hyperventilating and speaking rapidly; it had nothing to do with me. "Pugg, I've got some good news. "We are moooving." I didn't want to say or do anything that would reorient his euphoria. "DeMarie? DeMarie? Are you there?" I was returning to the dreadful reality that my life was about to change AGAIN. This time, would it be for better or worse? Part of me instantly discerned a shift in the atmosphere. This time, there was no tunnel vision to follow. No dreams, juuust the pit of my gut. I wanted like hell to help him find whatever it was he was looking for in life. I was smart enough to know when a person is displaying actions that may seem unjust or not quite aligned with what we would assume to be "normal" encounters between humans. There is something more extensive behind the actions.

As a young girl raised by her father, I took a few seconds to decipher what was going on before I finally responded. Deep down, I wanted to die. I was becoming good at acting as though everything was okay. "Cool. Okay, do I get a room?" I purposely set that question up while wondering which way he would respond. I was way ahead of the thinking game. If he said, "No, you won't," then I knew we were moving in with another family. "We'll talk about it when I get home!" he said, stumbling over his words. He abruptly hung up. I was happy he did shiiiit!!!!!.

Suddenly, my stomach was turning flips. I hurried to our room in the basement to pack my clothes. With a parent like mine, you've got to think ahead. I knew I needed to be ready before he got home, which meant one hour tops. I was soooo not feeling this right now. An array of thoughts were beginning to pour through my head. The only thing I could think to do was pray and talk to GOD. "GOD, I come to you asking if you could help me one more time. I promise I will try not to be so needy. Can you make sure that everyone will accept me for who I am? Can you please protect me from harm's way? I feel like something bad is happening. I also want to pray for Poppa. Please send him another good lady like the last wife he had. Lord, I know that things never work with him because of me. I don't want to be a burden on him any longer. They can look after me and give Rodell a break if you send him a good wife. I know you won't let me down. Amen." That always seemed to ease the pain. However, this time it didn't work. I continued to create an ocean around me, hoping it would carry me to the Promised Land. Anguish was brewing from a place unknown. I mustered enough strength to pick myself up off the floor, followed by a bathroom visit to stare myself straight in the face and spew all the hatred I could. "You are worthless! Your mother didn't want you. You're just a waste of..."

Before I could finish the question, "Why are you here?" I began to abuse myself. Rage-filled slaps ran across my face, followed by connecting punches. "Nobody loves you anyway." a sinister voice would say. "Do everyone a favor. Why don't ya!" questioned the *ID* in my flesh again, "Now wait a minute, can't we think about this?" I love you. You'll be okay, I promise." Those words could only have come from my purest side, *THE SUPEREGO*. However, the *ID* won. I looked in the medicine cabinet. Nothing! I proceeded to look under the sink cabinet. I closed my eyes and picked one. Bleach it was. I rehearsed my final goodbye to myself with more SELF LOATHING. I put my hand over the top of the lid and began to unscrew it. I got it completely unscrewed and the cap tipped over. It hit the floor in slow motion. It was almost as if someone had knocked the lid off! "Pugg, you in there?" His knock was indeed echoing in the hallowed bathroom. My throat closed on me just as the words formed. The Clorox left its calling card all over the floor.

I had air in between my words but the words steady. "Be...beee out soon. STUPID! STUPID!! STUPID!!! I smacked my forehead with the palm of my hands, and washed my face and hands. Then I gave myself a fake pep talk. "Act normal. Act normal. Act normal." Gripping the door handle with my clammy hands, I came out as if I never had a total meltdown without minding the Clorox smell that followed me. "Hey honey, how was your day at school??" He would ask as if he cared. "Good!" I replied. This was a typical answer coming from a kid who was from around the way. "Are you all packed up?" How could he had expected me to pack when he never told me to do so? "Yes, I did." "Well, let's go then!"

See, I was a misunderstood child from the beginning of creation. How could I not be? The womb I was growing in was swimming in the nutrients a baby needed to grow, yet fermented with the hatred FOR Paige from her mother. Generational elements passed down through DNA lay dormant—her womb filled with the sour drum of yelling, fighting, and constant crying. The umbilical cord wrapped in the heartache of all Paige yearned after. Paige was the epitome of inherited loss. All these LIVING words we had been suckling on in the womb of Paige. Unconsciously passed down, we had no idea what awaited us past gestation. Some people on my father's side knew my situation but turned a blind eye to me as a child. What I mean by that is that if you see that a little girl has an absent parent, do better for that child. Ensure she gets what they are supposed to have to be a decent human being. A child should not have to have a barbaric experience. Please don't sit back and talk about their hair not being combed when, in fact, you have no intention of fixing the problem. Give them **new core belief words and experiences to replace the negative thought patterns**. I believe this is why I couldn't fault my peer/cousins. I tried to love them even though I was made fun of for not having a mom, looking rough, not bathing as I should, etc.

Trembling took over me, and water filled my eyes. "Can I go and say bye to my cousin?" "Suit yourself." "Cuz, you know I'm moving, right?" She didn't say a word. She slowly nodded. Her eyes were a little glossy. I knew then through all the quarrelsome fights we may have had and all the hurtful things she would say. If anyone knew my story, she did! She held my face late at night while I cried for Paige. It was her who sat up late at night singing songs with me. Songs like SOMEWHERE OVER THE RAINBOW.

"I will miss us making up dances in the front yard." I reminisced as we hugged. "Kicking it at the community centers," she followed up. We were kicking flavor in the "T" before it was "Town Business." Getting money too. We stayed fly, just in case we ran into a cute guy! "Drinking, smoking, laughing, hanging out on your roof." Yes, I'm stalling. She dragged it on a little longer. "Let us not forget beating niggas and bitches up" We hugged as if we would never see each other again, which reminded me of that scene from COLOR PURPLE. We must never part (followed by handclaps). We were together every day, in every way. We both found courage and parted ways. I was finally ready for whatever was in store for me.

On the ride there, I was low-key pissed at him without a solid reason. I had a valid reason. I was tired of being dragged around. I had changed school twice a year, bouncing from home to home and car to car. YEAH!!! I was mad as fuck. I can remember a super long drive. It was a few country miles away. My Seattle heads from the CD

(Central District) to Downtown Renton. Back then, that was far.

At the time, it was the beginning of summer. It was a big apartment complex with hella people hanging out, playing music, drinking, and smoking. I remember being welcomed with love and compassion from this family of seven from Phoenix, Arizona; they consisted of a mother, Karen, and her sister, Patricia. She had some mental disabilities, and Karen took good care of her for those reasons. The oldest son, Larry, was twenty-five; the second son, Leim, was twenty-three. The third, Laurence, was seventeen. The fourth, Linna, who was the only daughter, was fifteen, and the youngest, La Donis, was eleven-year-old. La Donis and I shared the same birthday; October fourth. However, I was a year older. My first impression of them was of a close net family. I thought they were the new blaxicans (black & Mexicans). Most of our meals consisted of a Hispanic dish, just like the one I was welcomed with; Enchiladas. They were happy as hell to have me, even Linna. It turned out she always wanted a little sister. The mom was the sweetest lady I had met, and was funny as hell.

Everything was funny to her. In fact, the whole damn family was funny; even Patricia had a good sense of humor. I still don't know what's wrong with her; she just wasn't capable of running a household of her own. The good vibes and fun continued to grow. As time passed, nothing about the vibe changed. Shopping twice a week was right up my alley, considering the fact that Poppa didn't buy me clothes. Karen also made sure we stayed praising the Lord! We would attend all services and join the choir. That was where Rodell met her. In fact, that was where he met his women. Rodell started being the most upstanding father as their mom was to me. This shit was going great.

One day, arguments between the adults about adult shit started. I suppose they were good at keeping it between them for the most part. At that point, the air became thick. So much so that they were contemplating divorce. I was hurting because I knew where that would leave me; shit creek again. School trips ended up being long talks about my dad's drinking and not working. I was confused because that's what he got up early and dressed to do. I kept all the things I had been through in life to myself. I didn't want to run her off. One day, she took me to get sized for a new bra. Then she told me some things that broke my heart. Those things make me livid the most. She said my dad had told her many lies about me, like I was a problem child, to watch me cause I steal, was messy and a liar. I admit I had some deep-rooted shit going on. I was none of those things, which is why I was livid. My father would totally and completely tell lies about me to get a woman. So, now I understood his MO… to play the victim and have women feeling sorry for him because he had to be a single parent taking care of his child, who was a problem child to him. My heart grieved those statements, but I used another wall to hold myself up from melting on the floor. My thoughts were boiling at this moment. "Who do I have now?" I knew when we went places together I was used to getting the ladies' attention. For some reason, women liked single dads with a daughter. It was always that "woe is me" in a good way! I didn't mind that, but lying and saying unrealistic things about me to others wasn't cool. Momma Karen grabbed me, held me, and said, "I don't see that in you, honey. You are a beautiful young girl with great manners. I've never seen you steal things from any of us." In the beginning, because of who he portrayed me to be, I was investigated without my knowledge. I was constantly checked on. A spectacle, if you will, viewed under a microscope. My soul weighed against a feather. Yet, I had no clue. At this point, I was glad that I showed and proved myself. I wasn't that kid he portrayed me to be. What he did to me without my knowledge was deceitful. I was used as bait all my life. I've been a victim of his inherited debt. Those types of things open up the floodgates for things to happen to you based on things your parents have done. BOY, Rodell gotten himself into some tangled webs (I could go on about everything he has done. This book is solely about my journey, so I took out some things to keep y'all focused).

Later that night, I began to drink and smoke. It helped me stop the pessimistic chatter. I began kicking it with all the older people my big brothers hung out with. They never really handed me anything, but they never told me NO. They knew the dysfunction when they saw it, especially as it came from their own dysfunction. I was truly intoxicated and staggering to the house to take a leak. I was a tomboy at heart.

Saying things like taking a leak was totally appropriate. That Hennessy got me fucked up. I held mine at almost thirteen. Stumbling up the stairs to get to my apartment on the second floor, I swiftly opened the door. I scanned the living room and found ono one in there. The apartment that was once a nine-person home, filled with memories, laughter, love, and quarrels was turning very cold. Everything seems like a lucid dream. I hurried to the bathroom, standing with my legs crossed and my hand on my crotch to make it settle. As I exited the bathroom, I felt a presence. I stood very still with my drunk self. Trying to let my third eye pick up what I was feeling, my intuition failed me due to my intoxication. One thing for certain, it was a familiar presence. Then I came to my senses knowing that everyone would run in and out of the house all day and night. I had nothing to worry about! Shrugging my shoulders, I grabbed a soda and proceeded to my room. After slamming my soda, I laid across the bed on my belly. I began whimpering about Rodell and how it felt like God kept taking everything from me. I felt myself slipping into a weed and alcohol-induced slumber. Have you ever slept and felt like everything in "reality" is happening in your dream? I recall my bedroom door slowly opening. I felt a breeze of cold air brush past my cheek and I tried to get up. After a few effortless attempts to get up, I was unable to do as I must have fallen into a night of deep sleep. At some point, my spirit checked out. I was now watching myself as I laid across the bed lifeless. That overwhelming feeling I felt a while ago had returned. This time IT felt hungry. IT stood over my limp body. IT smelled my hair, followed by a very tempered touch to my lower back. My spirit was yelling at my flesh silently and tapping myself to wake up. At the same time, I was being tapped lightly to see how deeply asleep I had fallen. It all felt like a nightmare. Part of me knew this was no dream. The monster awoke me when I felt his unwanted, undesirable hand.

Pulling down my pants to the trail that leads to my forbidden fruit and with a jolt, I screamed "Nooooooo!!!!" Granting me access to my body, I sat up so quickly, panting and palpitating hard as though I was asthmatic. It was dark in my room. I look around, but I didn't see anyone. Was this just a bad dream? Why would I be having a crazy dream like that? As soon as I caught my breath, I stood up and turned the light on to clear my mind. But I hit the floor, flat on my face. My pants were to my ankles. At that moment, I knew something wasn't right with how I felt.

Before I could turn on the light, the monster came from under my bed. I knew because he stepped on my foot while on the floor. The monster ran past me and out of the house. I fixed my clothes and ran outside down the stairs still half intoxicated. All I could see was a short slue footed person running away. I found the closest wall to help me get my thoughts together. That can't be who I thought it was. I almost wanted IT to be some random person who walked into my house and really molested me and ran away. That wasn't my reality. I suddenly had a vision about Poppa's convo we had on the phone the day he said we were moving in. I felt something then and still had that same gut feeling then as I do now. I had just walked into the lion's den and was the bait.

The monster lived in my home and memories were flooding my mind. The beast had been watching me get my clothes ready each night to take a shower. Meals aren't the same. The gremlin never saw me as a "sister," and felt content with his actions. He knew NOBODY was checking for me, so he got in my underclothes drawer. He had been touching and seeking a fragrance that would remind him of my pheromones. I know this because certain items would be either missing or in the wrong drawer. I also wasn't allowed to have a lock on any bedroom doors. He watched me crush on guys and get all dolled up to be around them. This monster knew my every move. My daily rituals were never private. He knew how many brush strokes I used at night when doing my hair. Right before my eyes, I was being stocked like prey in my own home, and this monster lived under my bed. Rebellion was in my cards only if nobody would listen. What will I say? How will I say it? NO, NO, No!!!! That isn't going to work! What proof do you have that these things are happening to you? "Maybe you deserved what was being done to you?" a hateful sinister voice would say. In reality, children and teens didn't have a voice until someone decide to step in and believe the victim. One night, my bone-chilling voice shrieked with terror as I was being woken up from sleep by the monster under my bed. He would either use his hands as a violation instrument or his dirty, vile mouth. I had no clue my elixir of self-medicating my sorrows wasn't helping my GOD-given intuition at times. I would try to scream and ask for help, and fight him. So, by causing commotion, I thought people would "wake up" and not leave me ALONE with my night terrors. Sometimes someone would wake up and ask what the fuck was going on. "This motherfucker has been under my bed touching me while I was sleeping," I would say as I cried. "He would touch my private parts as well as put his mouth on me." I was hysterical, frantic and confused. Most notably, I now felt dirty. You could hear the pain in my voice. "Oh well" was the impression I got from almost everyone in the house at one point. Rodell also knew, but he didn't do anything. How could one not feel any heartache as I was pouring my heart out and trying to tell everyone what he was doing to me? During the day, everyone, including myself, went on like nothing ever happened. For me, suppression was the name of the game. I wasn't afraid of him during the day, but would feel helpless at night. I convinced myself I wasn't being raped and forced down on the bed. My most precious gift torn from the force. Bruises on my body, ripped clothes, and shit like that, but I was expected to keep quiet. This abuse went on for three years. It wasn't every night that I experienced abandonment, helplessness, being afraid, feeling stupid, terrorized, and a coward for not doing more to save myself. At the time, it wasn't necessary to teach your kids how to react to abuse in any form—I was never spoken to about how it wasn't my fault that these terrible things happened to me. It most certainly was swept under the rug, and not mentioned.

At the beginning of 8th grade, we moved to another area. Loving being a young teen at the tender age of one month shy of fifteen, I knew I had to take a stand. I kept trying to get someone in the house to hear me. Now the movement had gotten to outside family and close friends. This particular night, we had a dance at my school and I was able to attend. It was a twin dance and I was ready to go. A group of our close friends wore matching outfits; we had white T's with our tag names on the bottom backside. So, the white T's were worn tucked in the front and the back hanging out with starched-up blue jeans. Jeans so crispy that they could stand alone. With the left leg worn up, we had a TLC vibe. I had big glasses with dark make-up and two Lady of Rage afro puffs. On the day of the event, Karen dropped me off at school. She told me where to meet her after it was over and wished me lots of fun. From the moment I opened the car door, I was in my zone. I felt so fucking good stepping out of the car and feeling like a superstar. I was going to show out this night, especially as there were a couple of guys I had my eyes on. We did dirty dances; we did the freak dance to show which girl was more flexible and could do gymnastic style freak dancing on a guy, with girls, or by self. If you were good, you would be surrounded by your peers while they cheer you on "you better put it on him, girrrl!" My homegirls would yell, "You better tear his ass up and have his legs shaking!!" Hhaaa haaaa haaa!! We also had homegirl time but this time was to tease the dudes with sexual bumping and grinding. Being a lesbian wasn't popular when I was coming up. Then we would make up a routine step to some rap music. We chanted our gang name and threw our setup with our rags in our hands, as the music played on. The night was moving fast, but the visual was in slow motion. Before we knew it, our three hours of fun was over. Normally, you would either end up with your crush's number or jacket by the night's end. I walked up to the pool with my friends, laughing and cursing. "Biiiiiitch, did you see how I made Davon almost wet his pants? He took off running to the bathroom." I laughed so hard that I almost hit the ground. We are enjoying each other's company, hi fiving, smoking cigs and passing back and forth a bottle of Southern Comfort. They stood around with me for hella as I was waiting to be picked up. Then I tried to find the nearest payphone to call someone and figured that she had fallen asleep. No big deal. My friends lived within walking distance, so I walked to my friend, Sarah's, house. I called her severally but there was no answer. By this time, it was already midnight. Sarah woke up her mom to give me a ride home. I got home feeling like a motherfucker. The lights were ON, which meant someone was awake. I said bye and thanked Sarah and her mom. I got to the porch and grabbed the screen door handle, and I immediately got an instant mirage where I went straight on my knees and was crying. I also appeared to be packing clothes. I was instantly jolted back to my reality. I knocked on the door and it opened. Then I was snatched by my arm into the house. "Get yo fast tale asss in this muthafucken house!" Karen yelled. "Where the fuck was you after the dance, huh??" Swats from a belt followed. I was pissed, so I couldn't saying anything. Finally, I yelled. "Get... the... FUCK off meee..." I was where I was supposed to be. You... never came. Ask my friends," I said with tears running down my cheeks. "You lie, you little hoe!" she yelled. "I bet you were laid up with some pissy tale boy...wasn't you? Swat! Answer me." "I'm not lying! "Karen, why are you doing this?" I was starting to think Rodell gave her permission to do this to me. She had never treated me this way before. I began to feel like they set this whole situation up, and I screamed, "Fuck all you punk bitches in this house! I hate all of you. I wish you douche bags die." If ever my words had life, tonight was the night. My word became inflamed and I thought to myself, "Where the fuck is this so-called daddy of mine?" I started throwing shits like magazines on the table. I turned into the Tasmanian devil, breaking glass cups, and grabbing anything I could get my hands on to break or destroy. Then I called out to my father, "Rodell Rodell. Why are you letting her do this to me?" I'm telling you the truth." At this point, I had already lost my voice from screaming. I didn't give a fuck about anything. See, at this point in my life, I made it a point always to be honest no matter the situation. I kept screaming at him. I later realized that he was just lying there almost lifeless. Something took place while I was gone. This weird energy was bigger than me. "Poppa! POPPPPPPPAH!! Why can't I just go live with Paige?" I begged from the depths of my soul. Karen and I saw her at the mall, and she looked like she was doing well. She was believable because both my sisters moved back with her. "I don't want to be here any longer!!!! I CAN'T BE HERE ANY LONGER. IF YOU DON'T LET ME BE WITH PAIGE, I'M RUNNING AWAY. I've been TOUCHED for the past three years. None of you miserable people want to believe me. I can't stand to look at none of you. Do you hear me talking to you?" As for Linna, I couldn't even understand the dismissal. We shared a fucking room for crying out loud. Oftentimes, she would be woken up by my screams, sobbing and cries for some kind of protection. Linna started to get sick of my plea for help. One day, she caught him coming into our room on a particular night. She yelled at him, "Get the fuck out of my room and leave her alone!" She grabbed him by his neck and threw him to the ground. I was so happy to see this. I just knew people would believe me now. I've had to share every home with another family that had a young girl. Somehow I got the short end of the stick in one way or another. In this case. I was now considered the troubled child, and Linna the well-rounded child; the poster girl. She was super tall. She stood five feet eleven inches long with runway legs. She had a beautiful smile with dimples, good hair, and four-point zero GPA always. She also played hella sports. We genuinely loved each other and had a normal sisterhood. We also had usual disagreements, which were more fun times than bad. As Linna and I got older, they often compared the two of us. I was never allowed to be me. My favorite color was black, but anytime Karen bought something for me, she would say, "You get pink cause you're just a little girl." But

Linna got whatever she wanted. I didn't just get it. If I'm all these things, then I'm that fuck up of a child. "I'm telling you that I'm being molested in your home. Why won't you just let me go?" Rodell finally sat up. He looked me dead in my honey brown eyes and yelled, "NOOOOOOOOOOO!" It was intense. My hair on my neck stood up. I felt the floor underneath me rumble. I did a dry gulp. I was petrified for a brief second. "Why???" I screamed back. Finally, Karen stepped in. "Rodell, you can't keep that girl from being with her mother. If that is her wish, let her go." "You stay the fuck out of it. She is my muthafucken daughter." "Nigga you got me fucked up. I've been here, and she's my daughter too." Now the adults were arguing. "Well, I got Paige's number. I'm calling her tomorrow," Karen stated. Everything got quiet. I went to my room and laid down on my sister's bed. When you're the flunky or the youngest, you don't get to choose where your place is in a shared room. I went into the kitchen to get a knife and put it under my pillow. If this was going to be my last night here, then let's go out with a bang. Bwwaaahh ahhh haaaa! I was ready for war that night and also excited. I was older and I felt like I could take him on. I made sure not to sleep as the parent's room was right across the hall. I went into the closet to put my ear up against the wall. I felt like something else was going on. At first, all I could hear was whispering. Then all of a sudden, I heard him say, "Why didn't you tell her the truth? That you did all this to get her out the house." "You're not woman enough to tell her that you are leaving us?" "I couldn't because I love DeMarie," she continues to yell quietly. "I don't want to see her hurting because of me. I thought if I started to push her away, it would be easier to deal with." "With that being said, Rodell, you still don't have the right to keep her from her mother." "I'm not keeping her away!" Rodell said in a stern but slight whisper. "She can SEE her mother whenever she wants as Long as she's clean." "YOU heard what I said... I'm calling that girl's mom in the morning. "End of discussion." Karen deadened the conversation. Despite it all, I stayed up most of the night replaying my life with this family. I had to come to terms with this problem with La Donis. I knew I was getting the fuck out of here, one way or the other. I started to normalize and reason why he was doing these things to me. I wasn't his blood sister but I was a pretty girl.

I was weak because I didn't know how to stand up for myself.

Did he know that about me? Nobody loved me enough to step in. He was the only one who didn't want to be my brother and I started to respect that. In a sense, I thought this was my fault. Everything I got in life had to be karmic; my bad always outweighed the good. I came to grips with it now that I was leaving. But this doesn't excuse him; it meant that I won't allow this to continue to take over me. I knew I'll never be the same as constant night terrors plagued me. With this heartache pill in my mouth, the size of an antibiotic, I took a deep swallow. I pushed my "pain" pill down to the pit of my stomach. I decided that I would forget about it. I was even trying to tell myself that he was a young boy, so he might forget about me and get over his stepsister perversion. At about four or five in the morning, I began thinking about stupid stuffs like, what will I call her? Will she be nice to me? Do we have a lot in common? Scwwwwweeeeeeeek! I heard the sound of the door. As someone was trying to open the door quietly, I slept with the door barricaded the best I could. This gave me time to quickly turn over on my stomach and put one hand under my pillow. I was so scared that I could feel my heart about to explode from the palpitations. At this point, I began to sweat, as my body turned on its natural cooling mechanism. This got my pillow soaked. "Forgive me, GOD, because I'm about to sin" was my prayer over and over again. I tried to relax every muscle in my body so he would think I was asleep. I even started a little fake heavy breathing. I started to feel the normal ritual of shaking me to see if I was knocked out, and I gripped the knife even harder. In my mind, I was biting down on something and the anxiety was beginning to set in. then I began to feel his hot, sweaty, heavy panting ass, breathing by my ass and sniffing my private parts. As soon as he moved, I was on his ass. Bitch ass nigga! I was hoping to end it all right then and there. Then he moved. I pulled my arm from under that pillow so quickly! I didn't say a word, instead, I just focused on fucking him up. Slice! I got him. Yes! I got up and chased this bitch ass nigga out of my room while he was yelling like the bitch he was. "Momma...momma... momma come get her; she's crazy. She's chasing me with a knife. Momma!!!! Please, somebody help!" All I saw was RED. I was going to butcher his ass and feed him to my neighbor's dogs. I sliced his once alive skin as blood dripped everywhere. I began to yell shit like "NEVER FUCKING AGAIN! DO YOU FUCKING HEAR ME…ENOUGH! I WILL FUCKING KILL YOU! YOU SICK FUCK!" Immediately, I heard abrupt staggering, crashing, and things falling. It was my parents. They rushed into the living room while I was waving around a butcher knife. I picked that very knife because it was starting to rust a bit. I wanted him to get an infection from his cuts and die. I wasn't a killer, but they were pushing me. Then Karen said, "What is going?" Before she could finish her statement, I was already screaming at the top of my lungs and talking with a fast tongue. Then he began to say that I was lying, just like he always did. "I was in the living room minding my business, and she came at me with that rusty butcher knife." "Oh my gosh! You stabbed him." "Oh my gosh! You're crazy. I can't believe you." Yeah, it all appeared crazy. I was the one holding the bloody knife. I felt an urge to laugh. Then I began to whale out a laugh that was part sinister, part hurt, and part happiness. I knew this action would cause the adults to make a move. I didn't know where it would land me, but it had to be better than here. Besides, they were secretly preparing to split up anyway. Karen rushed the sucka to the hospital, and I had to clean up the house. Shit was straight out of a movie; specks of blood splattered over the walls and furniture, and pools of blood on the floor. I couldn't believe it came to this. I totally snapped. I felt something come over me as I looked around. I got a taste of what it was like to blow the fuck up. I had a natural high from the adrenaline rush. Euphoria! It was an amazing place to be. Poppa quickly snatched me by my arm in the blink of an eye. At times, I don't believe he knows his strength. I was sure his death grip on my arm would bruise me. "Can you let go of me? I didn't do anything. He's been hurting me for years." I said while he was still grabbing and shaking the shit out of me. "YOU LISTEN TO ME AND LISTEN GOOD. YOU HAVE BEEN A RED THORN IN MY ASS. I KNEW YOU WOULD GROW UP TO BE A BLACK ROSE JUST LIKE YA MOMMA. PACK YO SHIT BITCH CAUSE YOU GETTING OUT OF HERE RIGHT MOTHER FUCKING NOOOOOOOOOW.

And HURRY the FUCK UP!!!!" He shoved me toward my room. I paused and stood there for a minute. "I HATE ALL OF YOU. I HOPE YOU PEOPLE GO TO HELL." I slammed the door behind me, only to open the door again. I reached down in my soul. FUCK WHAT Y'ALL BELIEVE ABOUT ME. FUCK YOU GOD, FOR LETTING THIS HAPPEN TO ME. NOW KISS MY ASS! I wanted that to seal the deal on my vexation!!

THORN FIVE

Paige Wright's skin is just like the color of cocoa bronze. She wore her hair in very short curls. Sometimes the color in it would make her skin glow. She has deep brown eyes that could put one under a spell. To set off those eyes, she was blessed with dimples so deep you could store quarters. Her body was of an Afrikan goddess with small boobs and waist. My mom loved her jeans painted on, so tight if you blink, you might see two of Georgia's most delicate peaches in her pants. When she walked, it was easy to see where the trail of that peach began. Paige has such a peaceful aura about herself. She would give the shoes off her feet to someone in need. She was also known for not taking shit from anyone. She would have a day she would call "BAT

DAY." Anyone who owed her money or had a problem with her, it was a time to speak up. Paige had a quick draw kind of tongue. She was already coming for me, but Rodell didn't want this to happen.

Paige and her man named Dough came and got me with the little bags I had. I was so happy the nightmare with the monster under my bed was over. I ran up to Paige and hugged her so tight. I didn't care what she had done or how long she left me to suffer and endure my pain. I didn't care at that moment if she didn't hear me calling for her. I didn't care if she knew very little about me. I didn't care if she did not ask me about my life. I didn't care if she didn't have an apology waiting for me with flowers and candy. All I cared about was that it was REALLY her in the flesh. I wanted to learn her smell, to examine her and see what we had alike. This move wouldn't be for a short visit but forever. Even my fourteen-year-old self knew that we would have to learn each other. I just didn't care about any of that. It will come with time. We got to the apartment and I was the last to enter. I stood there meditating on my new life. Sometimes objects thrown in your path are meant to throw you off your predestined course. When a negative word attaches to the trauma, it sends out a magnetic field that tells the universe to pick me, which yells "I want more trauma!" In my opinion, if we can't learn at some point in our lives to take those ***CHIEF THEORY THORNS (CTT)*** and quiet them by sitting in silence (meditative state) and being aware of what we are thinking, the ***CTT*** will continue to show up in similar forms until we recognize it and turn it into a positive, followed by a positive visual to attach itself. Repeat this until your body is at ease; repeat it for life. When we are in gestation phase to being kids, our ***CTT*** and negative experiences are passed down because we are in the purest state of consciousness.

Rodell sheltered me from life. I suffered in many different ways as a child. Most of my heartache was mental infliction. To me, it is more deadly than a wound that won't heal. At this time, I also blamed GOD for the constant loss of love in my life. I knew it was GOD'S fault for taking away people in my life. It had to be; I was a child. I was standing before the door, sending myself down a rabbit hole of thoughts. My attention was grabbed by a vision that wanted my focus. I embraced the energy so that I could receive the message. My mom and I seemed to have a stare-down in what appeared to be a kitchen. I have never experienced multiple visions at once. As quickly as that one left, another came. No relation. During most of the time, my siblings were separated; I never got to see Ivonne. I now know my siblings went through a lot too. Ivonne was on his own at maybe twelve or thirteen, and was living with my grandmother. She took care of some cousins as well. At least ten kids were living there consistently. Some of my cousins had been with her since birth. Faye Wright was all they knew. Ivonne and Davine were the older two, so they would leave or run away. From what I understood, the favoritism was apparent. Ivonne took to the streets and was nicknamed "Too Tall". He was just too damn tall; he was called ***TOO TALL*** just for that very reason. He had stood six foot three inches tall by the time he was sixteen. The kid looked like he stood on stilts. He was blessed with those dimples that Paige has, and was most definitely of MOORE descent. He had reflective bronze skin and cocaine white teeth that are perfectly placed. By the way, no gaps or cavities. Those almond-shaped brown eyes would summon your attention away from those perfect teeth; they were startling. In fact, the boy was flawless. If you get a chance to be in his presence, you will see the love percolate around him.

People were mesmerized by his aura. All you can do is smile. Until he speaks, you will continue to be in a trance. When Ivonne didn't smile, it was a reason for worry; it was as though he could crush your soul with his eyes. Don't look too long, or your soul might disappear (sinister laugh). Paige raised Ivonne to be his three sisters' protector no matter WHAT. In this vision, Ivonne, Dakota, and I sat on a living room floor with poured-out bags of crumpled-up money. I came to reality, noticing I was still standing in front of the door. I was disoriented and weak. I opened the door and collapsed.

What a beautiful place, my home! I felt like I belonged here. When you opened the door, there was a cozy dining area and kitchen to the left. In front of me was a long hall. To my right, a vast living area with beautiful light color floral print sectional furniture adorned the enormous living area—

a sixty-inch flat screen (floor model) TV. I took a tour of the apartment to get the feel of things.

Last but not least was my room. I shared it with Dakota, my sister. I was very nervous about being in her space. Dakota and Davine were already living there. I just didn't want to make her mad or upset her. After all, we had never lived together. She already had it set for me where my things would go and where my bed was. I can honestly say that GOD did hear my prayers all these years. I was bubbling, but I held my composure. My mom was called my name at this point. She wanted to lay down the rules and what was expected of me. I was so excited to have chores and responsibilities. It was not the same as being treated like Cinderella, the rejected child nobody wanted.

I was going to take on those tasks with pride. You see, there was more to the way I thought at the time. I felt like I had to earn my keep, then maybe she won't throw me away. I wanted to show and prove that I could adapt to their program with ease. We didn't have a curfew. Mom just wanted to know where we were and to check-in. Both my sisters were in high school already and I was expect start high school the next September. Dakota was happy to let me hang out with her and her friends. I was genuinely grateful for this. I had left all my best friends and my boyfriend behind. For sure, Dakota is a brown girl. Just so you don't get it twisted, let me give you an example of the origins of brown. Brown represents a natural earth color that offers a feeling of strength and resilience. Brown is warmth. Brown is the tree root. Brown can invoke psychological reactions that can change how people behave and feel. The depths of her brown definitely lead us to the lands of Ancient Kemet. She has convex eyes that are a smokey chestnut on a winter morning. Dakota often had voluntary and involuntary expressions of happiness, pleasure, and amusement. She was a humorous girl who sought attention and love from those around her. Almost too trusting and loving. She loved her slick ponytails with lots of scrunchy hair ties. This style brings out the black beauty marks on her face that were ideally placed by the bottom of her lip and cheekbone. Her beauty marks highlighted her skin tone. She was blessed with the gift of gab, very social, outgoing, and a comforter. She couldn't stand it if she weren't the life of the party, and more so just to be able to make others happy. The need for affection could cost her one day. One particular day, Dakota was getting dressed. I usually would wait for an invite but this time, I knew that I would miss out on something. I would watch her as she was getting dressed. She had a sense of style that was beyond her. She loved baggy jeans, t-shirts, and Gap hoodie pullovers. I loved my sweatsuits and tracksuits. Dakota turned to me while combing her hair.

"I got some things to do today. You coming?" So eager to say yes, I spoke too soon and stumbled over her words. "Sure, I am." I already had in mind what I would wear. She did my hair; she put it in a side ponytail like hers with gelled-down swoop bangs. She put eyeliner on my eyes and black liner around my lips. Hella lip gloss. Just like I like it. "Hurry and use the bathroom so we can catch this bus." We rushed out of the house to catch a bus right in front of our apartment. I only rode the bus with her when we were at Granny Faye's home. We would smoke some weed, talk shit about people, and find ugly people to call each other boyfriends. We would also laugh, sing, and dance—anything in the name of laughter to take our mind off our family's dysfunction.

Dakota and I started seeing Paige less and less. She and her man, Dough, were having some problems, which we had no clear details about. On this day, we were out doing some extravagant shopping, thanks to Dough. We surely didn't ask questions though but I did know he was from Chicago, and he had survival skills, a street smart and could talk a cat off a fish truck. He was good at attracting money, which was all we cared to know as teens.

As soon as we got to Northgate Mall, I believed he felt something in his spirit. He handed my mom his wallet, then I told her he would be right back. He walked away quickly, almost a slow jog. One hour had passed, "Hey, ma?" "Dough hasn't come back yet?!" "Should we be worried?" I said in a panic. "Yes, we should!!" Paige begins to inquire, "Well, maybe he's waiting in the car." We finished our purchases in a hurry.

We were headed for the van when we saw the Seattle Police Department. The parking lot was surrounded by men on suit with guns drawn around, scopes out and dogs barking. Everything was moving in slow motion. We all looked at each other petrified. We were speaking to each other without saying a word. Paige told us to go on with our plans assuring that she would catch up with us. She handed Dakota a stack of money, and we hugged and parted ways. Dakota and I went to the ladies' room and changed into our new gear. We hopped on the next bus and headed to Skyway.

Off to Granny's house, we went not saying a word to each other the whole ride. Once we got to Granny's, all that was unspoken on the bus, was temporarily forgotten. We were embraced with love. In the Wright family, it was essential to show love. Love among every person in the house; from the matriarch down to the babies. We dropped our bags off in the garage. The older cousins were responsible for cleaning the house before we could leave. Most of the boys didn't "have to" but would. The older boys would be looking for their fit for the day, while we girls would get paid to iron their clothes. White T's with starched, crispy jeans or dickies were some young gangstas' attire. It couldn't be anything other than some G-Nikes or shell top Adidas and K-Swiss to dress their feet.

My niggas only hang with dudes on the same shit they on. If it didn't make money, it didn't make sense. If you are a Lil scarecrow, you couldn't be a part of "The Family." The Family was some groovy ass niggas, who would risk it all to keep their secrets. If somehow a snitch comes in the circle, it was clear to the community those kinds weren't welcome. The guys in this Family considered each other cousins. The cousins could range anywhere from about eight and up. Most of the big cousins came from other states to establish and set up shops. All the little cousins learned how to run the streets. For sure, some inner-city terrorists. Who wouldn't want to be like the Big Cousin?

The guys were driving nice cars! Swag is crazy through the roof. They were always dressed in the most exclusive wears. Layers of gold draped their neck and hands, everything looks so easily obtained. To a kid who comes from nothing, having something is everything. Some of us will cross a mother fucker to eat.

Those are the streets. These little dudes were nothing to play around with at a young age. It was evident that all they wanted to do was get money, have bitches, party, and most significantly, protect "THE CODE." It always appears that parting was most important until a rival tested a gangsta. Everyone carried a tool and bulletproof vest. Loyalty and honor were a must. We girls always joked about being a part of the "Family" at a young age. We liked the style the guys had. We would rock their Royalty colors; purple and white, of course. One pant leg up (left to be exact), and purple flag hanging out of my pocket.

In the early nineties, most guys had a jerry curl, while the ladies had long hair with braids or waves. Naturally, we were happy when our cousin Ricky Rich asked us if we wanted to come to the block to "hand out." It was a no-brainer what he meant. In our minds, we made it. Old enough to indulge was just what we craved. It suddenly felt like a holiday! Initiation day!

We hopped on the bus thick—at least seven of us, all blood cousins. Taking up the back of the bus, we made sure people understood. While on the back of the bus, we owned shit! My cousin Keema rolling blunts for us as we passed a bottle of Hennessy around. All the older cousins showed us sacred handshakes. They were impressed that we already knew them. Shit, we had been secretly practicing and we also got acquainted with greeting other Royalty Family members (formal language was necessary). The most fun to do was the signature dances. Putting creases in my brand new all-white K-Swiss was worth it. I knew I belonged. I knew my blood was purple. Loaded feeling free. Can't nobody tell us shit! Yelling ROy-AL-TEE before we got off the bus. Rich gave us one rule to follow! WATCH YOUR BACK!!!

Not a single salt grain of fear in us. We got off the bus READY, feeling invincible. The other cousins (Royalty Family) greeted us with handshakes. "What that ROYALTY like cousin?" was the greeting I received. Most of the "cousins" I already knew. All these guys are usually up at my Granny's house. It felt amazing to be greeted, though. I didn't need to be "put on" since I was born into this shit, affiliated. I felt the love I'd been missing my whole life. Whenever I was ready to take "that" step, the Royal family was always prepared. However, if I couldn't stomach the streets, I would be turned away and never allowed to be around in the hood.

A crackhead approached us, asking for Rich. "Aight, y'all, I'll be right back." Rich knew if he didn't make that jug, someone else would take his money. I remembered the rule he gave us. In contrast, everyone was laughing and telling jokes but I was watching my surroundings because it was getting dark. The darker it got, the better my intuition. With all the activity going on; nigga's running back and forth, making jugs and a group of nigga's shooting dice in front of the mini-mart.

Next to the store were some apartments, a village of a-z. Across the street was Andy's Bar-B-que Spot, which was always open twenty-four hours. You can get whatever you like; food, bitches, re-up, etc. House after house filled the block. All the places are identical brick, with about fifteen to twenty steps to the top. Well-kept bushes filled the hill that led to the top stair. At the top of the stairs, a concrete walkway separated the cottage-style homes. The homes faced each other. Lots of tall trees and more bushes dressed these houses.

While taking pictures with my mind, I noticed a guy standing at the end of the block, leaning against a light pole—with hazy eyes. I blinked, and the silhouette was gone. One of the homies was seen hugging everyone when about to move around to a different spot. He hugged me, and his long hair blew across my face causing my mind to spiral, in that millisecond. I immediately felt weak seeing my K-Swiss lying in a parking lot in front of some cars. I sat on the curb in front of the store and pulled out my blunt. I was praying over what I just saw, knowing I can't say anything. Who's going to believe me anyway? I looked up at Andy's, and the same silhouette I saw moments ago was back. This time I could see that this servant of the devil has a chopper. I quickly stood up and opened my eyes wide, but the nigga started spraying before I could turn and yell, run.

Everyone scattered in what felt like a slow motion. Some of the homies with pistols grabbed their guns. Protecting everyone was the shooters' job. A bunch of us ran in the same direction. It was smokey on the block—eerie tension in the air. A couple of our guys ran to the bushes to grab semi-automatic weapons and told us to be quiet and stay low. Scanning our surroundings, we saw a punk ass nigga jump in his car. "RUUUNN!!" echoed the air like a siren. They were shooting in the direction of the car while we ran. My heart was letting me know she was working overtime. My fight or flight had kicked in seeing that this batman black cutlass was gaining on us. I looked back to see how close they were; close enough for me to look down the barrel of their guns as they hung out the window. Pop! Pop! Pop! We all hit the corner and turned into the apartments. I was running alone and praying God spares my life. I felt my shoe strings loosening.

I was scanning the parking lot, looking for a place to hide. I looked back again and saw them coming for me, I started feeling like I was really about to die for this shit. Part of me was ready to meet GOD! After all, I should have been dead. The car stopped, turned off its lights, and revving its engine. I was running, trying to keep my shoes on but I lost my grip and stepped out of my shoe. I slid underneath a car, drowning in a mud puddle. Hell, I didn't give a fuck if it was piss at this point. I just hoped they didn't see any of us.

Who the fuck am I kidding? We are all about to die. I could see the tires of the car creeping. There is no way they didn't see me get under that car. I was driving myself crazy with my thoughts. I saw my shoe lying there just as I saw in the vision. The vehicle continued to creep through the parking lot. It was so quiet that I could hear the throbbing of everyone's heartbeat in tandem. The heartbeat spoke of the reaper in the atmosphere. Feeling like the coast was clear, percussions of our hearts and minds brought us back together.

We should have taken our asses home. Twisted dysfunction or not, we weren't letting anybody run us off our block. Silent fear turned into rage as the family reloaded. We walked across the street. Firearms were visible. We were completely drained, so we headed up the stairs to sit down. Niggas were standing at the bottom of the stairs, ready. Mothafuckers were pissed. Yelling and screaming filled the air. This led to arguments between the guys about people not doing their job and how it just cost us.

"Ssshhhhh! You don't know if these foo's are gone. Be smart until we can make a move."

Before I could say anything else, I heard something in the bushes, "Yooooo, do yall hear that?"

I made eye contact with the enemy. I saw a pair of eyes in the bushes, "Ruuuun run!!!!" Blending in with the night, the dude hopped out of the bushes dumping. I was one of the first people to get to the top, so naturally, I ended up being the last one down the stairs, ducking and dodging. Praying and weighing my life, AGAIN. The streets I call home were indeed reminding me that I would die out here. Going down the stairs, our shooters were coming up. I looked back and saw the nigga who once terrorized our block leaking. His blood soaked the steps. He didn't get hit without putting a slug in one of the guys.

He collapsed in the middle of the street. Crazy that he was the one hit. He was right in front of me, going down the stairs. I watched him lay in the street. My mind glitched as I saw myself spread out on the pavement. My "purple" blood collected around my body, "Yoooo my nigg you good?" "He alive, Royalty!" "Let us get him to the hospital." Riding in a blue 1986 Chevy Suburban with tinted windows. We some boyz in our hood.

It was a good night in our minds because we didn't lose anyone. We pulled up to the best trauma center on the

West Coast, Harborview Medical Center. We were waiting outside, chopping it up about what happened.

The Big Cousins called a meeting. The ladies were invited (it's a must). I felt accepted with a prideful smile, a part of the family. It was simple, I lacked love, and they showed it despite all that happened. I watched how shit was going down while on the block—facing my next blunt—picturing myself with stacks! I planned how I was going to get the loot in my head. Becoming a self-made millionaire was my motive.

The nurse came to tell us that he will walk away with his life. The cost of this thug's life will remind him; the bullet lodged in his back will forever remain. If he grows an inch or that muthafucka moves, he will be paralyzed. Does that stop a real G?

Listening to DUBEE Mackin was my duty on our way home, followed by MACDRE Game, I'm spittin. Those songs confirmed the gangsta in me. We made it to Granny's. Muddy as hell, in a crazy way, I was in love. I was looking down at my clothes. I reminded myself the life I have was covered in dirt and stains. It was far sadder than the fantasy I would create for myself thuggin.

Fucked up, we fell asleep on the floor in the garage. At exactly 6AM, my Granny woke us up yelling. If anyone knew Granny Faye, she was the FAX LOCAL NEWSPAPER. She mainly looked at the paper to see the posted obituaries. Granny and her ten children knew everyone in the town, so word traveled fast. She knew what took place last night. She woke us up with some not-so-Granny-like words.

"BIIIITCH!! Get yo asses up!" Ricky was the oldest cousin living with Granny. Naturally, he was the first "bitch" to get in trouble. Granny started swinging her belt, "You cock suckers (the girls) don't have no business out with these fools! I am calling Paige and telling her! As a matter of fact! Get ya shit together; y'all need to go home!" We didn't give a fuck what she was talking about. We were immune to a cussing, fussing Granny! Did she have a right to do it? Maybe. Hugging all the cousins that were awakened by the yelling and laughing it off, "We'll be back tomorrow, ROYALTY!!" "NO, YOU WON'T! AND STOP SAYING

THAT ROYALTY SHIT IN MY HOUSE!!" out of love, we always aggravated Granny! "GRANNY, YOU STARTED THIS ROYALTY SHIT! YOU ARE MAMA ROYALTY!" endless laughing as we exited the house.

Dakota and I walked down the hill in the morning dark. From Skyway to Burien, we go. Burnt out, we couldn't wait to get in our beds.

Dakota opens the door to be greeted by Paige, "Sup?" I didn't know what to expect. I was new to Paige's way of discipline. "Momma told me what happened! I wanna hear from y'all what happened?!" Since Dakota was older, she was looking to her to explain. Here, we were in trouble, and this Lady thinks it is funny. Paige was smiling extremely hard. Her Amusement was almost artificial. She let us know she wasn't mad with us. "Go clean up, and get some rest. We'll handle this later."

I couldn't process if I was in trouble or not. I was concerned Paige would throw me away like everyone else.

Body dry as a prune, so I headed to the kitchen for a cold drink. Paige was in the kitchen with her back turned. I must have scared her from the way she jumped. I couldn't explain the feeling coming over me, but something wasn't right. I looked down at her hand, and they were knuckleball tight! She slowly turned around with the biggest grin on her face. I was focusing my eyes, trying to channel my intuition. Then I continued to the fridge. In that split second, she turned her back again. This time I heard a lighter flicker, so I quickly closed the refrigerator. She turned toward me and released a fat cloud. She inhaled every bit of that cloud back in before it dissipated. I was standing here shell-shocked. This was the very moment I internalized what was going on with Paige.

It broke me down seeing a glass pipe in her hand filled with resin. I met Paige's kryptonite. My eyes filled with tears as that pipe spoke to me and said, "IT IS I...CRACK COCAINE! I AM HERE TO GIVE PAIGE A TEMPORARY EUPHORIA THAT WILL DESTROY YOU ALL! AS LONG AS I'M AROUND, YOUR SUPERWOMAN WILL FOREVER CHOOSE ME!" A haunting voice laughed. This laugh came through Paige. Noticing she didn't give a damn about what she just exposed me to. Numb as a bitch. I fought back the tears, turned and went to my room. She never said a word. I would forever be *traumatized* by the *dysfunction.*

THORN SIX

We come from Seattle, WA. It is a middle-class town compared to notorious places like Chicago, Los Angeles, New York, and Louisiana, etc., with higher crime rates, drugs, and poverty. Seattle is a beautiful place. Full of mountains that paint the horizon.

Bodies of water are of the most authentic blue. Spring enough to drink from the water hose.

Most importantly, I can't leave out the beautiful trees that help give us the Emerald City name. Many opportunities to raise a family are endless. Decent public and private schools are scattered abroad. Unless you come from nothing like many of us, one would have to take a magnifying glass to my city and see it hold its own skeletons. Many of which we lived every day. Drugs, gangs, poverty, imperfection, generational curses, and police brutality are wrapped in cognitive dissonance. You name it; it was plenty to see. Bipolar weather can change from snow to rain and sunshine in a few minutes, which can naturally cause some chemical imbalance in a city that doesn't have many recreational things to do.

Today, we moved our belongings to a town far from Burien. I glistened inside, knowing we get to start over. We would reside at a four-plex on the corner, bottom right to be exact. As we settled in our new home, we began to experience a different kind of belly ache. Something in the air reeked of malfunctioning elements, layers of broken, flawed, debilitating *belief systems*. The *dysfunction* always starts sweet.

Paige started work at Mel's Market in downtown Seattle. She loved her job so much, and she brings food home almost daily. I saw hope in her eyes. A strong Black Woman was radiating through her despair. I felt the security blanket wrapped around me, causing me to relax. My protection wall was coming down. We were finally a family operating on a "***normal dysfunctional level.***" It didn't take Dakota and me long to meet people. We already introduced ourselves to the neighbors. It was a breezy eighty-nine degree, and we were outside trying to check out what we could see. We walked to the closest store and ran into two of my Best friends from middle school, Miracle and Tree (treeona). Miracle is a long-legged beauty who is gangsta but girly when need be. Tree is a little shorter than me, and she has long, wavy hair with an illuminating and infectious smile. We hugged, and I introduced them to Dakota. We found out Miracle lived a block away from us, so we all walked home together. Miracle filled us in on who lived in the neighborhood. The three of us were inseparable. You would never see us apart. We made a pact that we were more than best friends. We were SEESTERS 4 LIIIFE!!!! We vowed that nothing or nobody would get in our way. A sister handshake would seal the commitment we made to each other.

Dakota is so talented at many things. At the time, she loved to write rap songs, and she was great at remembering lyrics to some of our favorite fast-talking, quick-tongue songs. She blessed us with a couple of bars she wrote: IT BE THOSE CRAZY BOMB ASS RIDERS FROM THE BLOCK TWO FORTY FOURTH, PUTTING IT DOWN IN YOUR LATE TOWN WITH THOSE ROYAL GANGSTA'S FO SHO, STRAIGHT STOMPING ON YOU HOES THAT WANT TO HATE ON THE GAME, BITCH RUN UP AND GET DONE UP ON YO BACK IS WHERE YOU LAY! Couldn't anybody tell us shit? Not ever the girls on the other side of town that we didn't deal with. We didn't like this other group of girls because we suspected we saw the same guys from the hood. We also felt; that, naturally, we were the prettier of the groups. In our minds, that was enough to have "Beef" with the girls. We knew that showing the guys we were on what they were, they would always put us before any hoe-ass bitch. We let it be known who we were at parties and barbeques. Our anthem was straightforward everywhere we went.

Another SEESTER would join the group. Her name is Tammy. Tammy was just what we needed to even the load. She was a beautiful indigenous Mexican and Black girl. Long hair and dimples were her outstanding features. She also went to middle school with us. I was the first to befriend her and brought her around the girls back in middle school. Tammy showed herself approved because she was just like me. I once was the new girl in middle school and did not know the others that had already been rocking for years. The girls in school would assume she was automatically scary, but not my bitch Tammy. She came in swinging. That girl can throw them thangs.

The four of us spent most of our days wearing matching clothes, smoking weed, drinking, and chasing the guys. Tammy would soon introduce her cousin Analise to the group. I was not too fond of her energy from the day I met her. I couldn’t tell why I was instantly angry. Hanging with Analise the first day was coo. I just couldn't put my finger on why she made me angry to be in her presence when I didn't even know her. As long as Analise was around, she would always get the side eye from me. Miracle's friendly ass would always tell me I was tripping. I started to think that too, like maybe I'm a jealous best friend. As soon as I let up, she was not just stealing my best friend; she was stealing Our SEEESTER! Miracle and Analise would drift away from the group more and more. They did things solo, even found boyfriends that were best friends who weren't from our hood. These actions were a violation of the gang we ran with. This behavior triggered some anxiety, but I had much bigger problems in my life.

I walked into the house to use the bathroom, then I heard a subtle whimper come out from the master bedroom. I saw Paige sitting on the floor with her hands covering her face through a cracked door. She reached over and picked up a lighter and a glass stem. People who used crack would buy the glass stem from the corner store which ironically comes with a *rose* inside. The *rose* was discarded and replaced with brillow and crack rock.

Paige was having a conversation with her kryptonite that only the two understood. She noticed I was at the door and motioned for me to come in as she hid her pipe. With chains around her tears, they were slung to the floor with force. Paige was a badass chick who rarely cried. I watched her swallow her pain, letting me know she was let go from her job. I knew how much she loved her job and how happy she was to provide for us. I also knew she would find a way even though she had a charge on her record that would keep her from getting any job she wanted. I wrapped my arms around my mommy so tight. Thunder and lightning started as our bodies met. I saw a three-day notice in my vision, but it didn't scare me this time. "It's going to be okay, mommy. Dakota and I can help out!" "No, I want you girls to finish school and go to college."

"Don't worry, let me!"

I hit Dakota up on her pager with nine one one-two forty-four. That meant meet me at the stop sign in front of the house right now! Dakota showed up with Miracle. I shared with them what was going on. Many solutions came to mind, but I also wanted to do as Paige said. I can admit I was embarrassed because, once again, our friends had everything we wished we had. Miracle had no reason to be running away from home and doing everything she was doing. Most of the time, if she ran away, it was to our house. My mom would cuss her out in love but still let her stay. She always encouraged Miracle to go home after a couple of days of being over and eating up our food. I always wondered why. She had it so good. Miracle knew we had been under a lot of pressure these days, so she stayed around the neighborhood to hang with us even though she just got off of house arrest. "Hey, let's go hand with one of the homies; he just hit me up and asked if I wanted to smoke!" "We can get some "work" (crack) from him so you guys can help your mom." Dakota and I looked at each other and smiled, let's go! Paige came outside and walked past us. Whether she chooses to smoke crack or not, she is always clean. Her hair was usually done with matching clothes from head to toe. She always smelt so good; this time, Paige's aroma was covered with a loud stench of grit and grime. In pin drop silence, the three of us watched Paige vanish.

Before we could get a tear out, there came Diablo. He was the head of one of the many branches of the Royal family. This session would be Dakota's and my first time meeting him. Judging by his appearance and many scares and tattoo's on his face, the tag name was definitely fitting. Diablo was a very nice guy and had plenty of jokes. I started to notice he liked my sister, "You sure are beautiful. How old are you?" "I'm sixteen." Diablo reached out to her and kissed her hand. Dakota was about to throw up, but she knew she couldn't be disrespectful to a niggah named Diablo! "Hey y'all smoking or what? Hop in!" the back doors to his Ford SUV swung open. We looked at each other for confirmation before racing to get window seats. Miracle and Dakota got the windows, while I was seated in the middle. "I've gotta get a pack of swishers first so we can roll up!" "I hope y'all know how to roll!" We all yelled I DO!!

Diablo stopped at the store, passed us the swishers and a quarter pound of weed, and said "Roll it all!" We were like some kids in a toy store racing to see who could roll the most and perfect blunts. After the third blunt, I realized we were nowhere near our home. I nudged Miracle, "Where the fuck is he taking us?" She shrugged her shoulders in disbelief. Diablo passed me the blunt, touching my hand in the process. That exchange was enough for me to feel the negative energy radiating. The exchange came across as fear. I felt in my gut that the three of us girls were in some trouble. Maybe I was tripping. I was loaded, so maybe what I was seeing wasn't accurate.

I looked in his rearview mirror only to see him watching me. I gulped so loud hoping he didn't hear me. We locked eyes, and I swear this man reached into my soul and pulled out all my fears to slap me with them. Not taking one eye off me, he says, "I have to make a run to the other side of town. Y'all good? Or do we need to take you, little kids, home? "Nah, we riding!" We all say in unison. Although I could sense that something wasn't right, but I proceed anyway. We were on the sixth blunt when Miracle made a song request for Brother Lynch's Situation On Dirty. That put me in hustle mode, emotions on high. I felt invincible. I couldn't wait to discuss business with the girls and Diablo. I was certain he had connections if he wasn't the connect himself.

After about an hour's drive, we were starving. We convinced Diablo to buy us something to eat. Did we use Dakota as bait? Of course we did. As long as Dakota sat in the front seat, he would agree. Devouring our food, we ignored where we were going. High rise apartments sat in front of us. Diablo got out and told us to stay put. We sat in his truck for two hours, wondering what he was doing. Complaints of being hot and needing to use the bathroom suffocated the truck. Dakota noticed Diablo and a woman looking out the window at us, then quickly shutting the blinds. “Fuck this shit. I'm going to the door,” Dakota says. “You bitches coming or what?” BAM! BAM! BAM! Damn! Dakota bitch, beating on the door like the damn police. Miracle says looking at us while laughing, “BAM! BAM! BAM! BAM! Biiitch! If you don't stop beating on these people's door!” Before I could finish, a fat, greasy-looking hoe answered the door. Miracle stepped up, "Aye, is Diablo in there? Tell that foo he forgot about us!" "Fuck all that I need to use the bathroom!" Dakota said. "Please, please let me use your bathroom?" Without a word, the girl let us in and locked the door with a key. “It's dark as fuck in this bitch!” Miracle says. "Yo, turn on some lights." "I can't see shit!" Dakota follows. "Shhh! Be quiet; you're going to make him mad. He doesn't like lights here." She turned on a light, told Dakota where the bathroom was and asked us to follow her. “Sit here, and I'll be back.” After a few minutes passed, Miracle and I were wondering what the fuck was going on. Dakota hasn't come from the bathroom, and the girl hasn't come back with Diablo. "Let's go find Dakota," Miracle whispers. "Yeah, she has been gone a long time." Before I could say anything else, the girl came down the stairs and said he was coming. Dakota followed, holding her stomach. "Man, that food fucked me up!" "Fuck bitch you could have let us go first!"

"Anyhow, my fault, girls. My name is Kim. I am Diablo's baby momma." As she sparks, a blunt rolled in a Garceir Vega as a peace offering. We looked at each other and smiled, knowing we were ready to smoke again. The blunt smelt necrotic, like the reaper, rolled it. Kim puffed puffed and passed it to Miracle, though nothing really fazes Miracle. I took my hits and passed it to Dakota. We were good. Maybe the blunt stank because of the bammer she was smoking. The next thing I knew, I was melting into the couch; everything around me was melting too! I tried to tell myself to stand up, but my body wouldn't move. My mind was talking to me; 'stand up bitch! You dummies are in trouble now. Didn't you get the signal I was trying to give you?' I was staring at the front door as if my telekinesis was going to open the door. It might have been possible if my soul wasn't sitting beside me, just as soggy as I was. I remembered I wasn't alone. Dakota was reaching for the air, trying to grab something. Miracle was on the end of the couch, yelling 'fuck you bitch. You got meee fucked up!' She must have realized the bitch set us up. The fat greasy bitch Kim was gone, and it was extremely cloudy in here.

Diablo finally came downstairs. He grabbed Dakota by the neck, "YOU BITCHES THINK YOU GONE SMOKE MY WEED AND EAT MY MUTHA FUCKING FOOD LIKE I'M SOME KIND OF TRICK ASS NIGGAH HUH?!" "Y'ALL GOT ME FUCKED UP ON ROYALTY, MY NIGGAH!" Kim pulled out a gun and pointed it at me. High as a giraffe's ass, I couldn't comprehend what was actually happening, until it had already happened. My spirit guide was sleeping on the couch while I stared down the barrel of a gun. Knees knocking, I was grabbed by Kim and held against my will. A thunderous voice said, "Let that hoe go before you kill her. If you kill her stupid, she can't give me my money back." Diablo threw some clothes at us. Pissed that she couldn't shoot me, Kim shoved me to the ground. The stupid bitch dropped her gun. Shooting Diablo in the foot. Miracle grabbed the gun and pointed it at the both of them, "Let us go, and we won't hurt you or tell anyone. Kim? Open the door bitch, NOW!" "Yeah, Bitch!" Dakota would follow; "If my brother finds out, he will kill you niggah!" Diablo asked her who her brother was, and she was very proud to say "TOO TALL!" My brother's name rang bells in our world. It didn't surprise me that he knew him. "Kim, let these bitches go!" Kim grabbed the keys and opened the front door not before I could grab the gun from Miracle and telling her to tie the niggah in a chair with his shoe strings. "I don't trust this, foo! Kim, get yo bitch ass over here too." Miracle and Dakota tied them to a chair; there was blood everywhere. We didn't care though. "Now, I'm not leaving until you tell me where the weed, money, and dope are." Miracle and Dakota pulled up the floor and took his stash and gun, and also took his truck. Miracle was the only one who knew how to drive, thank God! She got us back to the highway. We dumped Diablo's truck, doing our gangster dance down the highway. We didn't care how far we had to get home, we were just happy to be alive. Things would have been worse if it wasn't for Dakota saying Ivonne's name.

With a name like Diablo, he certainly would have returned for us. Throwing up are gang signs. We felt good. Watching our back, ready to shoot anyone who looked suspicious. We finally hit the block. The sun beat us home. Splatters of blood on our clothes. We knew we had to go to my house to change and split up the goods. I was stopped dead in my tracks as I couldn't believe my eyes! My heart fell out of my mouth to the ground as I looked at Dakota. An ocean flooded my vision. Dakota walked over to me and held my hand. It was a long walk to the front door. Everything was moving in slow motion. I saw all the neighbors outside looking like hecklers, but where the fuck is the ambulance with my stretcher?

I distinctively noticed my clothes scattered throughout the parking lot. I looked to the right; there were dishes, bathroom stuff, a dining room table, and chairs. To the left were more clothes, mattresses, and dressers. I even saw my big stuffed tweety bird, a padlock on the door, and an eviction notice that read we were trespassing if we entered the premises. We both dropped to our knees. Our souls exchanged an agreement that didn't need to be spoken. One of the neighbors came down the stairs and said we could stay there as long as we needed.

As we stood up, he told us to come upstairs to their place. We got upstairs and saw my big screen TV in their living room along with our furniture. To add insult to our wounds, the teenage girls had the nerve to wear some of I and Dakota's clothes. Conflicting feelings were causing a meltdown inside us. We couldn't let them see us sweat! The dad of the house upstairs told us that he had opened a back window for us. We spent the next few weeks in survival mode in this abandoned house. Going to the nearest grocery store, we would fill old bags with cartons of cigarettes, liquor, and enough food to last. We were desperately trying to survive without creating more bad karma for ourselves. We struggled to find someone who would open their doors for us! At this point in life, who the fuck needs a GOD or family or fucking bitch ass friends? All of a sudden, nobody knows us! Even the weirdos with all our shit in their house. Miracle also disappeared but later came back hanging out with Analise and the other girls. I learned a valuable lesson about "friends." Never once did any of the girls opened their door the way we had, especially Miracle who was with us the most. How could she leave us in a true time of need? She stayed with us numerous times. All the trust I ever had was gone. I snapped. I didn't trust myself no more. When you take away a person's livelihood; food, water, shelter, love, empathy, and funds, it can trigger mania. My emotions were masked with confusing laughter followed by nonchalant tear falls.

From one house to the next was all I knew from the time I could remember. I was staying at a cousin's house who had a nasty addiction to crack rock at the tender age of twenty-five. I was going to make the best of this situation. I finally clocked sixteen and was old enough for a job. I got hired at

Burger King. Optimistic about change, I accepted it. After a month of working and selling a little "dope"(crack) on the side, I finally had enough money to buy a car and even gave my cousin money for letting me stay. I got off from working a ten-hour shift and headed to my room. My feet hurt so bad. I couldn't wait to lie down. Hyperventilating, I knew there was only one reason why someone would kick in my door. The dope and money! Fuck this life! I had to leave. I moved into her house with barely anything, and now I'm leaving with less. I sat on the curb outside the apartment. Thinking about how if it weren't for my bad luck, I wouldn't have any at all. This is no time to weep. I must keep moving before thoughts of not wanting to live enter my inner matrix.

My cousin Keyma pulled up with my stepbrother Larry, they told me to get in the car and come stay with them at my stepmom's house. Keyma was staying with me at her sister's house, but her stuff was missing too. She also told me that her sister was being evicted because she was going to jail for a long time. I wasn't going to go because the molester still lived there. This time, my uncle from my mom's side of the family and Keyma's dad were in a relationship with my dad's wife. The circumstances didn't bother me one bit. I said okay because I felt secure knowing my gangsta-ass uncle would be living there. "I'm only going to stay long enough to get emancipated!" Like a moth to a flame, I was back in the twilight zone...

Faith

Complete confidence or trust in a person, thing, or concept.

My definition of Faith

Complete trust in myself and my spiritual connection to God.

3 Keys to applying Faith

1. You are choosing to have peace no matter the circumstances. Do what you can do. Don't worry about what you can't. Find a system for the solution.
2. Change your focus. Find Affirmations.
3. Feed your mind by reading books, coaching, conferences, workshops, and videos.

MY SON, forget not my law or teaching, but let your heart keep my commandments;

2. For length of days and years of a life [worth living] and tranquility [inward and outward and continuing through old age till death], these shall they add to you.
3. Let not mercy and kindness [shutting out all hatred and selfishness] and truth [shutting out all deliberate hypocrisy or falsehood] forsake you; bind them about your neck, write them upon the tablet of your heart.
4. So shall you find favor, good understanding, and high esteem in the sight [or judgment] of God and man.
5. Lean on, trust in, and be confident in the Lord with all your heart and mind and do not rely on your own insight or understanding.
6. In all your ways know, recognize, and acknowledge Him, and He will direct and make straight and plain your paths.

PROVERBS 3:1-6

THORN SEVEN

I strongly desired to try a different type of hustle. One that I knew wouldn't land me in jail—petrified and alone. My best thinking came when I was high. I called my brother, Larry, to give me eight wraps of weed; unbeknownst to him, he would have to let me borrow some money too. I was a desperado, willing to take from someone else's plate or anything to keep my head above water. I was seventeen and well aware that nobody owed me anything anymore. I took it upon myself to lead my own way.

"Yello!" "What's up, big bro! I was trying to come and meet you for some chronic." "Yup, I got you. I'm at the strip club on the highway, DeJavu, for my nigga birthday; come through." It's only fitting that I looked good going into a strip club. You never know who you are going to meet. I had long box braids down to my butt. My head-turning black leather skirt. I wore it with a neon purple glow-in-the-dark onesie top and light-up heels. One thing Paige taught me was to always dress the part. When you look good, you feel better. When you feel your best, you can attract the best.

In front of me were big pink flashing lights. With a fake ID in hand, I walked in with no problem. Charmed by what I was looking at. Flashing lights had me hypnotized. I couldn't believe my young ass was up in this bitch for real. I had to remember to change my hat; I was about to start doing cartwheels in the muthafucking club.

The vibe had me fixated on the dancer on stage. The dancer's body movement was in sync with the music. She controlled the atmosphere. She was a star in her own right. The customers loved what she had to offer. She was showing him the possibility of an exclusive, once-in-a-lifetime experience with her. An exotic fantasy is what she's offering. For some, if the price is right, you just might get your wish. Said but unspoken, he wanted the type of experience he can't get at home, so he paid for it here.

"What's good, Sis?" A dap and a head nod were all I was able to give. Soon as I sat down, there came a waitress. She must have smelt my adolescence. "Hey there, you're new here, aren't you?" "Yup" "I could tell by the way you watching her!" "I can see you up there, ya know!
You are a stunning lady. My name is Roxy, and that is our house vet Stormi."

Man! She had me when she said she could see me, little old me up there. That was it! The message was heaven-sent; I knew it and immediately accepted my assignment. But what would my name be? Roxy heard my heart speak. "RAIN! We'll call you Rain, Yeah? We have an amateur night every other Friday at 10 pm. You should come out this coming Friday." "Hey, Roxy, you can't be offering my lil sister a job up in here!" "Boy, shut up! Girl, don't let him stop your hustle."
For me to accept what I was about to do, I denounced any Godly beliefs I may have had. With his words infused, I was putting down my spiritual necklace. Any positive way of thinking was out the door. I was shedding all perspectives of me and creating who and what I wanted to

be. I took off my empathy earrings, my peace bracelets, and my ring of beliefs! Honey, I am ready for this new me.

The word got around quickly that I was entering the world of stripping. Friends and family were making arrangements to come see me at a local establishment called DUKE'S. Deja Vu just wasn't going to cut it, especially if I didn't want to be snatched off stage by my brother, Larry! I had three days to get my shit together. The only way I could gain knowledge about this world was to watch movies and late-night explicit rap videos and mimic the moves that these ladies had. I was a swift learner when it came to dancing; it was one of my passions growing up. I went to Lovers Package and bought whatever I could that was small and tight. Last but most important to me was the music choices. I spent the next few days going down to DUKE'S, watching how things operated.

The first thing I paid attention to was the clients that came through there. What they looked like, what kind of attire they wore, and if they do appear to be a working man, gangster, or bum? I was intrigued by the thought of what brings a man to these establishments.

I was aware of a gentleman who had been there every night I was there. I assumed he was a regular. He seemed to know everyone at Duke's. He was a very loud guy who clearly liked attention. I know his type. I mentally noted this and kept moving like I didn’t see him. I didn't pay him much attention until I walked by as he was getting a lap dance. He stood up so fast that the poor girl almost lost her balance. Before I knew it, he grabbed my wrist. "Beauty is your name, right?" He totally got the stank face for that corny line. "Uhh, NO!" laughing inside because this guy is a joke. I put my poker face on, even though I want to roll on the floor laughing. "UNHAND ME NOW! You Don't Know Me To Be Grabbing Me Like That Nigga!" As I was storming out of his eyesight, he yelled, "OH, Your Fiesty Just Like I Like Them, Baby!" I called me a yellow cab and got the hell out of there. In the cab, I was feeling my body going into full panic mode. He triggered a negative feeling that was attached to a "DNTP" file labeled 'molested growing up'. I shed a tear, believing I would have to deal with many men like this. I cried even harder, knowing if I didn't do this I won't have a legit way to provide for myself. A comforting voice sat next

to me and echoed, "TURN FROM YOUR WAYS AND KNOW THAT I AM GOD!" Call me a renegade. I am on a quest and no longer under any commandment of anything I can't put my arms around or call on the phone! I am a loner, and I will figure it out ALONE. Forgive me, Father GOD, in advance if I'm wrong about you and for my sins...
It was Friday, and I was one hour away from my big night. Mixed emotions, but I can't turn back now. Standing in the full body mirror, DeMarie, meet Rain, Rain, meet DeMarie! DeMarie looked at Rain from the feet up. French tip toes, check! Clear platform, ankle strap, open-toe heels. Check! Knee pads! Check! White mini tennis skirt. Check! Sexy white bra. Check! Glow in the dark glitter body paint! "THE BOMB BIIITCH! Time to move as a grown woman! Always Protect your Mind and Body." I hear the Dj calling for Rain. DeMarie scary ass waited behind the curtain until the song began. Rain, Shiiit! This altered ego of mine had no fear.

The beat dropped from JANET JACKSON'S ANY TIME, ANY PLACE. I swallowed that the house was full and all my people were front and center. I blocked it out and pretended it's just me in the room alone. Dragging my heels across the ground as I slowly entered the stage, and one hand on the glass mirror wall leaving my fingerprints and Rosey aroma trailing. Stopping in the center with my back against the glass, I could feel the light's heat warming me up as I rolled my illuminating five-foot frame over and over. Biting my lip as I slid up and down that glass wall, butterflying one leg at a time, followed by both, and isolating my pelvic thrusts in between. Tonight is the night I put all my frustrations right here on this stage. The ground was calling me. Cat crawling across the floor, wide open legs with an arched back. I was starting to get aroused by my hair whipping and body touching. I rose on my knees, caressing my hard nipples and perky boobs. As I ran my wet tongue across them, my head moved from side to side. I took my toes and pointed them upward on my back, admiring my heels. Bending the knee in a clockwise direction, I leisurely moved my leg bringing it around and back to the other foot repeatedly. Slow and erotic is the name of this game. Swinging and staggering my legs in a teasing manner. I loved how this "body art expression" was making me feel. I felt wanted, admired, and in a new zone. I could see my reflection in the beads of sweat starting to form all over my shimmering skin. I was so dedicated to this performance that I didn't notice the money falling around until I started making open clam circles with my hips. I rocked onto my back, put my legs behind my head, and pat all this fat cat goodness. Heels clacking the floor, making a sexy sound. Lying on one side of my hip came a whole body movement, head, chest, belly, hips, etc. Waves with my legs and heels, swiping, smooth slithering, and accentuation of both legs pointed.

Transition to the pole was a must. Being an amateur, I didn't know tricks, but I could make it look just as sexy! One hand was high on the pole as my body pulled away from it. A steamy sexy, seductive walk, dragging and making circles around the pole. The walk also gave me a minute to cool down while sliding my hands down the pole like it was a hard membrane. With opposition, I went into a few body waves. Leading with my head, chest, then my belly, pulling away while I bent my knees. On the tip of my heels, I ended up with my juicy ass glistening and poking out. I went into figure eights. One knee in and out, the other followed. I added the swaying of my hips. Before I knew it, I was naked doing a slow wind booty pop on a handstand. Right in front of the stage! There was standing ovation before my song completely faded. Cheers and screams as I stood there holding my clothes. I opted to go last so it could be memorable. It worked as planned because I won the competition, and they paid for my license to work. It was like a dream come true.

The first night of work turned into weeks of low pay, dealing with perverse men, and hating ass bitches. When I first got there, I was assigned a "house mom" whose job was to look after the babies of the club, teach them pole tricks and show them how the game goes. My house mom's name was Raven. She had been around for eight years. I was happy she picked me. I knew I was going to learn everything possible to make more money. At this point, I was dreading coming to work. I needed something to help me get through the degrading side of it all. I started drinking every night just to get through. Sober just isn't the way to do it anymore. After a few months of drinking every night, I realized I was consuming too much. I was sloppy, stumbling through the club and slurring my words. I would not remember shit the next day. Losing my money and fucking up my connection with the customers. Once I stopped drinking so much, I was able to see things for what they really were. My looking glass showed me that Raven was sabotaging me. The DJ would mess up my music if I got on stage to do my set. I could hear her snickers through the crowd. I was having things like old food being put in my locker and stealing my outfits. There was never a bouncer around to escort me out. I heard rumors from some of the girls; Raven was known for bringing in the young girls and turning them out. I didn't have the evidence to prove it, plus I wasn't worried about her. I knew I was headstrong and wasn't about to let some granny stripper stop my hustle. In my opinion, you can always count on at least three types of strippers. You have the bottom-of-the-barrel bitches I call FILLERS. The FILLERS never really do shit. They come to work to not work. When they do dance, they do the laziest job enough to get their drug fixed. These bitches take the most broke clients and turn dates with them for twos and fews. They are just there to fill spaces. Next is the HUSTLER or

HER~stler. She knows exactly who she is and what her goals are. She isn't easily persuaded. She has clear boundaries. The HER~stler in her sticks to her script. She meets her quota every time. Most importantly, she does not fraternize with the other girls who are bottom feeders. Lastly, there is what I call G'S, aka GRANNY STRIPPER. The Granny strippers are bitches who have worked the longest and will never leave for one reason or another. The G's are bitches who secretly desire a skill, talent, or even a certain look that one of the girls may possess. The G's have so much hatred in their hearts that it spills out, causing them to act out by sabotaging the ladies and setting them up for failure. Even death may come of it.

I truly believe we are all in Spiritual College, unconsciously taking classes every second of our day. Some spiritual lessons take longer while some can take multiple tries to pass. Some are effortless. When God has a specific assignment for us, we undergo trials to sharpen our skills, courage, faithfulness, and love. We can also go through trials when we turn our back on God by participating "IN" the world instead of following God's path for us. The further we stray, and the longer we are absent from God, we become necrotic. Dead inside! Yet! Only if HE (GOD) chooses to revive you will you become brand new!

I had my first good night in weeks. I was so happy. The bread just kept coming. That regular customer I told y'all about has been hounding me this whole time. I wouldn't bend or break. I wanted to carry myself as a hustler. All that bullshit disappeared when he offered me a thousand-dollar private dance. How can I refuse? He came with a Gucci bag filled with Bath and Body Works and white roses. I must have given him the dance of his life because the next day, Raven was blowing up my phone about the guy.

"Hey Raven, do you need something?" "Actually, I do! YOU" "What do you mean?" "That gentleman you dated yesterday wants a private night with you and some other girls. 9pm until after midnight. The other girls will be there for your comfort and to show you the ropes. Don't worry, six thousand dollars he's offering. The money will go through the house, and you will be paid four thousand. He wants to do it as soon as possible, so get back to me. Oh, by the way, I'm sure he hasn't told you his name?" as she laughs, "He goes by Trap. Click."

I was elated, I knew the money would start to flow if I stuck with it. Rolling my breakfast blunt of Purple Kush definitely got my mind going. If I can get clients like this, I will be set. Four thousand dollars is enough for me at eighteen to begin. "TRAP, HUH? HIZ ASS GONNA BE THE ONE TRAPPED IN MY MONEY SCHEME!! HAAA!! AAAHHH!" One thing that is certain is if he got six thousand to blow, there is more where that came from. I called Raven back.

"BITCH count me in! Fill me in on the details."

"This is top secret, so you gotta swear your loyalty!" "I swear!" "Duke's has a Passion House where VIP customers can pay for a no-sex experience. The house has three rooms upstairs; a massage parlor, a fetish room and a secret room I can't tell you about yet!" "The main floor has a movie room and kitchen. Downstairs is the pole room, and out through the sliding door is the backyard with a pool, hot tub, fire pit, and space to bar-b-que. There will be a contract to sign between all parties that states what's allowed and

what isn't. There are always two bouncers here at all times. I will be stopping by on my way home. Any questions?"
"NO."

The night came, and I was prepared for the festivities. I got there seeing everything was in place, just like Raven said. The precision was very militant. It made the hairs on my arms rise. I made a self-note that something was slightly off. I could be tripping, though. It was my first time; maybe it's run differently than they run the club. I was escorted to the kitchen, where a cook was making dinner. Trap was already waiting; he was very easy on the eyes. It was that easy to follow through with it. Baby vet was there waiting for the strawberry shortcake which was meant for dessert. As soon as I was served my bowl, I got a call from Raven saying she was sending a car for Baby and the other girls. A large birthday party had arrived. The two bouncers would stay there and guard me. Before I could say anything, she hung up. Gazing at the phone for a second in confusion, I had to pull it together as nothing was going to get in the way. I need this money badly.

"What did she want?" asked Baby. "Mmm, she said she sent you and the girls a car."

"It's almost eleven o'clock. It's time for us to get in the hot tube," Trap requested. I went to the bathroom, and got a call from Baby saying she wanted to say she is sorry and told me a couple things about Trap. One, she heard he secretly liked men. Two, he is less scary if you get him drunk. But she hung up before I could ask why. Oh well I got money on my mind, that's it!

Everything was cool; we were smoking weed in the hot tub. Trap was on a tangent about his life; how he owns a retail shop, sells drugs on the side and comes from a respected family in New York. I guess he needed someone to talk to for the night, and that's where I come in.

After getting out of the hot tub, he was ready for his show in the pole room. I called the bouncers several times, but nobody was answering. This was the time I needed them most. I can't have an aroused man in my presence alone, I don't trust men like that but the greedy side of me allowed me to dismiss a lot that night. As the night progressed, I started to feel more and more like I was hoodwinked. Fuck it! I had nothing to lose and everything to gain, including my respect after I beat these bitches' asses for lying and doing some shady shit. I had to go in my zone and kept reminding myself why I was here.

I love dancing to songs like Aero Smith, Guns & Roses, and Def Leopard. After my set, I took a break and headed to the bathroom to change into my next outfit. After changing, I opened the door with a deep exhale only to find him standing at the door butt hole naked, with his dick in his hand. I tried to remain calm as I didn't want him to know I was scared. "Hey, what's going on? I just went in the bathroom to change, and you are naked! This isn't part of our contract! We didn't include going all the way." "Bitch you can stop this nice girl, fasaid! I paid money for you. I paid for access to all holes, ya feel me." He doesn't seem like the same person I've been hanging with all night. Looking into his eyes, searching for anything I could pick up, I noticed his nose has powder all around it. Once his nose started to drain, I knew I was in trouble. He snatched me out of the bathroom, pulling at my clothes. I had to think fast. "WAIT! WAIT, PLEASE WAIT! Can I at least have a drink?" I couldn't believe what I was about to say, but I continued, "I see that you brought the white girl with you, and you not going to share with me?" Lord have mercy, what was I thinking? "Oh, don't worry, you were going to get high with me, rather you like it or not." While I was behind the bar fixing us a drink, I remembered Baby telling me she put Visine in my bag and told me to use it on him if he got out of line. She said to only use one drop to put him to sleep. Fuck that! I put four. This nigga is going to need a tranquilizer. While I was taking my time mixing drinks, Trap was running his mouth, talking about how he hates strippers. "Y'all bitches just the same as a HOE; you just don't walk the streets! Some of you are bouji and too stuck up!" I could hear the aggression rising in his voice. As he does a line, he told me he couldn't wait to get me back for disrespecting him in the club during our first encounter. I was shaking so bad that I could barely mix drinks. "So now what's it going to be, DeMarie? Are you going to give, or I'm going to take?" I dropped my glass on the floor in shock. How the fuck did he know my name? "Get. The. Fuck. Over here and stop stalling." "Oh! I'm not; I just didn't know you knew my name." I quickly poured myself a shot, threw it back and headed over to him. He grabbed the drink and pounced it. He then pointed to the lines he had separated on the table and gave me a rolled-up dollar bill. I exhaled and inhaled the powder through my nostril. I instantly felt the burning sensation traveling through my nose and down the back of my throat. It had a really unique taste, slightly like chlorine water. It made my nose and throat tickle and itchy at the same time. "AAHHHHH!" I grabbed my nose, trying to squeeze the burn away. The dopamine triggered a chain reaction that made me feel warm all over. It was so good that it knocked me on my ass. I was stuck for a few seconds until I felt this weird ass nigga forcing me to suck his little pink dick. I was tussling with him to let me go, he stood up and dropped his wallet. OH, MY. FUCKING GOSH! "Detective Evan Grayson." I said quietly. I was acting like I didn't know anything. Fuck! The coke was making me a little chary. Millions of thoughts ran through my mind, and I could hear all of them. The ones that spoke the loudest said, 'continue to play the role with him.' So, I got into character, rubbing his washboard chest. "I just want you to relax, Trap, and let me give you the salacious experience you asked for. We got toys upstairs if you want to play?" I could tell I was getting a rise out of him. I knew if I could get upstairs to let the bouncers know, they would kick his ass and throw him out. He nodded in agreement for me to go upstairs. One thing I did know ninety-nine percent of the time is that a man will risk it all for a nut; and not to have blue balls.

With repeated thwacks on the door, "Please! Please. Answer the fucking door." I kept looking back and forth; it was pitch black at the bottom of the stairs. I was petrified, knowing he was coming for me. Tiptoeing down the stairs, I was convulsing. I entered the main room, and "officer tricky" was passed out on the floor. I nudged him with my foot checking to ensure I didn't kill him. The more I kicked, the more I realized he was out. A wrist pulse proved he was alive but with a faint pulse. I ran to the bar to get my backpack. I had hair pins and a bank card to pick the lock. Not before I saw a disposable camera in my bag, I figured I should leave my calling card.

Everyone got me twisted. I rolled his clammy body on his back, put makeup on his ass, propped one leg up on the chair and put a condom in his mouth and ass. I took my mouse and spelt 'officer tricky' right in front of him, just to seal the deal. Officer tricky had a backpack also that I took along with his keys and wallet. Feeling triumphant, I vandalized everything I could on the way out.

I drove his car to the highway and went through it and his backpack. I found money in his bag and ecstasy pills in his trunk. I made sure to wipe everything down. Considering all I just went through; it has got me feeling ill. I started throwing up on the side of the road. Duke's wasn't far, so I walked down there. Of course, nobody I wanted to see was there. Sick as a dog. I cleaned out my locker and laid low for a while because I was confused and traumatized. I needed to devise a plan; shit wasn't over for me. I wanted my revenge. The following week, dressed in all black with a hijab on, I caught Baby coming out her house. I drove her around threatening to kill her if she didn't tell me what was happening.

"OK! Ok!" She replied as I smacked her punk ass with my gun. "It was Raven's idea. Raven is my mom. She has a pimp, and he is the club owner. "What the fuck!" I was blown away by what I was hearing. "Together they bring in young girls and trap them in the lifestyle. The club owner and Trap are best friends, so the three of them came up with the idea to trick you into working for them. They made me pull you in as well, I really didn't mean it. Trap said he was going to take our kids from me." "Yawl kids? Your baby daddy is Trap? Officer tricky?" "YES! I, too, was tricked into this lifestyle. I couldn't do that to you; you've been cool with me." "Show me where I can find Officer tricky." I sent a hood call to the Royal family for a favor. My guys didn't even have to show out. Word on the street, he got smoked on the job.

I soon after had a daydream. In that vision, I was pregnant. My visions are usually spot on, perhaps it was broken. God knew I wasn't going to believe it. He sent a funny-looking angel to speak to me in the middle of the night. The angel spoke to me about a baby girl God sent to change my life for the better. GOD sure has a way of getting my attention. I ran to the bathroom to do a line. I looked at myself in the mirror, surprised at the image of Paige I saw. At that moment, I glitched, feeling like I was becoming the very thing everyone told me I was all my life; exactly like Paige. After crying myself to sleep, I woke up the next morning almost late for my doctor's appointment. Dr. Sugar was talking about me being pregnant, but I assured her it wasn't possible. She knew that as well because she's the one who put me on Depo Provera. She made sure I fully understood that nothing is one hundred percent effective. I agreed to take the stupid blood work; sobbing and soaking my clothes in tears. "What am I going to do with a child?" I can barely take care of myself. A voice said, "I saved you from yourself!" A hysterical laugh came out twisted with a cry. This must be a joke. God really does have humor, to think a baby was going to help me. I was homeless, parentless, and clearly, my DNA said I was incapable of caring for one. At the time, I couldn't fathom abortion. I guess we are having a baby. Estimated due date of 10/04/2001. My birthday!

THORN EIGHT

Quotidian dysfunction is at an all-time high in my life. At twenty-two, I had a three-year-old daughter named Ahniyah. She was everything GOD said she would be. It was at this point I had a better understanding of what GOD was saying to me. Mentally, she was the inducement in my life. Seven was the number of times I moved around with my child. I needed a place to be when my eldest sister, Davine, offered her home. I was in no position to turn it down. Davine inspired me to be great. I enrolled in Eton Medical School. I had our future covered, but RIGHT NOW is what's crucial. The school was from 7am until 11am. I was sitting in my car down to my last, contemplating making a call.

I was telling myself I must prepare to put on my hustle panties when done with the call. When I looked at my dashboard, there sat a picture of my baby girl; that was the only reason I put it all on the line. I swallowed my pride and called my nigga yellow (Yella). "Yo! What's up, D?!" "What's good, Yella?" "You tell me, Ma?" "I need to see you." I didn't need to say much; he knew. Meet me at seven eleven on three twentieth and pacific highway, in twenty. He hung up fast. I learned how to get what I wanted from people. It didn't cost me shit but a smile.

Twenty minutes quickly turned into an hour. I knew the game, so I wasn't trippin. I was out of my element on the highway. The same concept was everywhere, I imagined. I was scared to death. I don't like asking people for shit. I was already beating myself up for not being in my own apartment. He finally pulled up in a black 2002 Chevy Tahoe, on the driver's side of my white 1999 Nissan Sentra. His beats in his car were thumping. I couldn't tell what was louder; my heart or his beats. He rolled the window down—motioned for me. "Aye, Ma, can you walk yo sexy ass in the store and get me a bottle of water and whatever you like." I had already changed out of my scrubs and into my booty shorts and tank with my flipflops. I hopped in his truck. He's a busy man, so whether I'm "sexy" or not, we both wanted same thing; the Money. He got right to it. "So, what's good, Lil mama?" "Maaaaan Yella!! It's all bad." "Say no more!" Glad he cut me off cause my ass didn't want to tell him everything. "What do you want? The soft or the hard?" "Well, all I got at this very second is a quarter of this hard." "When you are ready to re-up, hit me up!" I made sure to reach over and hug him tight. Smash my boobs up against his chest and arms around his neck. I wanted him to save my scent. "Thank you so much!! I promise I will pay you back!!!" "Naaaaaaa," waving his hand, "you ain't gotta do that!!" I returned to my car, knowing I would repay him in my heart. I didn't know how long it would take, but I vowed to keep my business clean.

I was so fucking pumped. I sped out of the parking lot going north down Pacific Highway. I got to about 240th and my car ran out of gas. I pulled into an apartment complex with about fourteen apartments—seven at the top and seven at the bottom. There was a gas station about a mile away, but I didn't have enough for a gas can and gas. I looked down at the off-white substance wrapped in a tied-up sandwich bag. It spoke to me, "I'm here to 'serve' you in ANY WAY you choose." I got out of the car and went in my trunk to see if I had a blade. There was no blade, so I got back in the car. The night was beginning to fall. Now was my chance to spot someone looking for some work (crack). All I needed was one person.

I grabbed my blunt and cigs and headed for the black holes of the night. I was looking for a particular type of fein; fast-moving and twitchy. Not well kept. Dark burnt hands. They had to be willing to hit it in front of me—Code of the streets. I knew from experience to hand out some of your products for them to try and wait; they were going to bring it back. I spotted a super short lady. She was walking mighty fast, so I motioned for her to come over. With the twitches, hand gestures, and constant moving, I knew all I had to do was slide her this good. "What's good, ma? I'm D. What's your name?" Barely able to pay attention or stand still; time was of the essence. "My name is Mecca!" While sweeping the ground with her hands. "Look! I'm new around here, and

I need someone to try this cream; tell me if it's good. If you know someone, let me know." I turned and walked away. She caught up to me so fast. "You said your name was D? I can help you with what you got." I broke a piece off of the brick with my thumbnail and I made sure she saw it. I gave her a crumb and told her to smoke it right before me. She knows the drill. She pulled out her glass stem. She inhaled and was on a good one. From what I understood, the high doesn't last long. That's where the chase comes in; she loved it. Now everything will come; she will bring me paying customers to keep herself full. I didn't mind. I made eight hundred off that quarter. Normally, it would have cost me one hundred and fifty dollars. I was so happy. I had to call my guy Yella. "Yoooooo Yella, thank you so much for what you did for me. I'm out and ready to re-up! How soon can you meet me? It's jugging out here." "It's good, Ma! I see you. What do you need? Same? All right!! Coo, I'm down the street from you; give a nigga a few minutes." I headed back to my car thinking how I couldn't let myself get that happy. In my mind, I was still broke. I took out the money to re-up, put gas money aside and left the rest in a slit I cut under my driver's seat. I will forever move like I don't have it. I'm not telling anyone what I got going, mainly because I'm a female. I didn't want to get caught slipping or some hater plots to get me. Davine was blowing my phone up. "Where you at, Girl? The daycare called me to pick up Ahniyah. I made dinner. Are you coming home?" "Yea, I stayed late at school. Then I went and fell asleep at my homegirl's house from school. I'll be there in a minute." I met Yella, he took me to get gas, and I took my ass home.

I continued to make moves in the same neighborhood. Every night I would do the same thing I did with Mecca. My buzz was cracken. Word gets around fast; I was officially a "D" Girl! Yeah! Dope girl Dee, I liked that. I had her circle of people sewed up. She hooked me up with a few people that were working addicts, boosters, and mechanics. Mecca used to get high with her mom, Denim. Denim seemed to be controlling. She sold Mecca to men to fuel their drug-induced habits. It was a party every night. I got so busy that I was finding reasons to leave school and meet people at the nearest store. Sometimes it was so good that I never cared coming back to class. I started having my friends cover for me and paying them to do my work. One of my home girls from class, Eve, came to me and asked me how I was making all this money. She said she needed to make some extra cash for her son and bills. She was a single mom from Denver, Colorado. She had been up here for two years, and shit was getting rough. She did have a sister that stayed in Poulsbo, Washington. I knew how it felt to need help. Fuck it, pay that shit forward. I put her on the first time, no charge. I wasn't close to being a big dog yet, but I was far from broke. I sold five, ten, twenty, fifty dollar crack rocks. Don't get it twisted; I didn't turn down shit but my collar. If you came with change, I got you! If you came with dollars, I got you.

I gave Eve ten fifty rocks. She could sell it like it is or bust it down and make more. Eve and I were becoming super cool; always on the phone or at each other's house. I even met her son, Gary, who was fifteen. I didn't see him much. He played sports or was with the aunty in Poulsbo. Evva and I were always going out to lunch for business. We discussed building an empire together, sitting in school, and plotting on classmates. We knew who liked that "White

Horse," and still covering for each other. Eve was bubbling fast. I patted myself on the back. She was way older than me; at least Paige's age. I didn't give a fuck because I always hung around people two and three times my age. Eve was meeting me a couple of times a day. Life was grand.

I had moved up in the game; I started buying that soft. I had to cook it myself though I'd never done it before, but there was nothing that was going to stop me from getting this cheese; not school, family, or even being a mom. I was on a mission. I had the mentality that Ahniyah would thank me later. I was having so much fetty. I bought a safe and a Glock 19 and buried the safe in a wooded area near a park.

The apartment building my car ran out of gas was the spot I chose to set up a shop. I was paying a lady who lived on the top floor. I called her "Lady B," I used her parking spot while I walked around the neighborhood making my jugs. I also had runners who would make money for me. I took care of everyone; fed them, and I treated everyone with love and respect as long as they stayed in line. On this day, I parked my car, ready to get out. Lady B came out and was going off about me parking here. She must have been hearing about my buzz and wanted some goods, so I thought. I felt I needed to keep it clean with her in case I needed to use her home for anything. I also knew she smoked big dope and always had parties. "Hey! Say, baby girl!! You can't park here anymore." As she was mumbling and slick talking. "My guy doesn't want you around here!" "Wait, what?" She now has my attention. I was always looking for opportunities to solve problems. I looked up to her window, to see someone hide. "Who the fuck is that in your window?" The rage in me was filling up. "I don't like people who know me, but I don't know them!" "Oh, that's Juvy!" "Juvy? What the fuck is a Juvy? Lady B!! That's how you are going to do me?"

"What do you want, more money?" I pulled out a hundred. "NO, I…I.I can't accept that, I will get in trouble!" "Trouble?" I knew just how to fix this. Whoever this is wasn't about to run me off. "Lady B, can I please use your bathroom?" "Yeah, baby girl, but make it quick." I locked up my car and headed to her apartment. I didn't knock or anything. I pushed the door open so hard that it put a hole on the wall. I scoped out the small one-bedroom about six hundred feet, the bedroom door was closed. It's cloudy as a muthafucka in here. I needed all entries opened before I could use the bathroom. "It's nothing to worry about, baby girl. My guy is in that room, that's all. I wouldn't lie to you." She went on to open the door. A young man was lying on the bed, acting like he was asleep. I gave lady B the motion to sweep the house for me; she did just that. I gave her a bag of crack crumbs, I knew she would find pleasure in it and would be under my spell soon after. I motioned for everyone to be quiet then I went to the restroom and locked the door. I waited in silence as I wanted to see if someone was going to make a move. After three minutes, there was nothing. I learned to carry a box cutter in my mouth from my hustle days downtown with Dakota. I walked up on this dude lying across the bed and tapped the back of his leg with aggression. "Yo! Your name Juvy?" He turned over. "Who asking? I am. What do you need, some work?" I was taken aback by his statement. To me, this means he was watching me. "Nawww nigga!! If I did!! I got my own plug. Why are you telling Lady B to stop me from parking over here?" "BECAUSE YOU ARE STOPPING MY MONEY!" He screamed like a Lil bitch. I knew that was a lie. I heard yelling, so I quickly moved to the living room. I don't know my surroundings at this point; I must stay alert. It was Lady B. "What's up, mamma, you good?" She was tweaking about how good that dope was. "Now see, this what I'm talking bout. Not that shit Juvy is selling." "Oh, baby, you have become my new Girl." I looked over at him and smiled.

I give Lady B my number right in front of the nigga. "You good?" I asked him. It looked like he was a little pale. "Breath, nigga." As I laughed out loud, I turned my back and walked away, but was always ready to pop this blade. At this point, I just marked my new territory in front of this dude. It wasn't a smart thing to do. But hey, it needed to be done. I got to my car and started it, and there came this foo!! I'm not crazy; I didn't roll my window down. "Wut up?" I asked him. "Why are you walking up on my car?"

"Can I talk to you for a minute?" I knew this foo was desperate at this time. I thought to keep him around because I was doing the most by myself. If I had him around, that would keep some folks from always seeing me alone. I felt like I had just gained an enemy; I must watch him. I got out

of my car to hear what he had to say. Sure enough, he wanted to work with me, I didn’t know about that. "What's your name again? Junny?" "BWAAAA!!" I knew his name. He's somewhat pissed; now I must play Nice Nasty!!
"Don't play, you know my name, Lord!!!" "Lord?" "Yea, I'm from Chicago!! I don't play that shit!" "Mmm hhhmmm!!! Anyway, this is how it's going to be. I don't trust you, soooo, I need to keep you around me. I don't want to be taken advantage of by these base heads and other street nigga's. I'll pay you. If you pass the test, you can level up." He agreed and we exchanged numbers. Before I pulled off, I told him this was his last time making money at my spot!!! My queen of hearts laugh said it all.

I asked for it, and I received it. Life was feeling better, little by little. Late nights and early mornings became even longer nights, followed by stretched days. I had to push myself even harder. Eve was working at a nursing home as a CNA. She put me on; graveyard shift was what I chose. I had to figure out how I could slip through the cracks of this position. I couldn't lose my clientele. I knew I could do it. I had a few people I could trust so far. The key to the operation was to take care of your crew. I never got much sleep. Suppose I could catch a cat nap at the nursing home, I would; right in an empty bed in one of my resident's rooms. I even had a few trustworthy working smokers stopping by the nursing home. Shit was starting to get serious with this Juvy kid. I wasn't seeing anyone, so fuck it! He's not as bad as I wanted him to be. I set traps for people, left thousands in my car and dropped a sac; shit like that. I already grew up not trusting a mother fucker. That will never change! Eve didn't work on the same floor as me, but we performed the same hours. Sometimes we would ride to work together. Once Juvy and I started spending personal time together, Eve began to regress a little. Rightfully so; I got a man now. Shit started unfolding with Juvy real fast. He mentioned he had a crazy baby momma who was obsessed with him. She always found where he was. It didn't bother me. Just don't get in my way.

I was still living with my sister Davine, trying to stack a grip. She doesn't appreciate my lifestyle. She did everything she could to change the narrative of her life. Davine was the eldest daughter. She was a split image of our mother, Paige.

She wore her hair in an asymmetrical cut and flat iron that gripped her face and set off her marquise-cut eyes—complemented by lips and a complete outline of a heart. She, too, is a bronze Sistah of metallic brown skin. Davine was authentic when she spoke. She most certainly came to play with none. If you didn't know her, the words that came out of her mouth would hit you like a 9 mm gun, looking for your head.

However, Davine didn't deal well with family-related pain or anything close to it, so she kept her petite mouth plugged with her thumb. This way, she could keep herself comforted. In contrast, she was pushing down the affliction with her thumb. Suckling on her agony was an indescribable taste and drowning in her belly was the thing in life that pledged her. Davine graduated high school and went on to Medical School. She didn't smoke weed or do any hard drugs; she was totally against it. It was a trigger. At this point, Davine became fed up with me. Ahniyah didn't want for anything. Whatever I had to endure, she would ride the wave with me.

I had plenty of boosters, gift cards, food stamps, cleaning supplies, etc., you name it. I came in with the agreement clearly stating that I didn't have to pay bills. It was only right I did whatever I could to earn my keep. Unconsciously, I was operating in an illusion. Everything I touched slipped through the cracks of my hands. Everything that was meant for you will stick with you. In my case, I wasn't supposed to have anything. I started on a mission to secure a consistent lifestyle for my daughter. In the midst of all these, friends of mine were now getting into stripping, using drugs, partying, and more. I never received accolades for the good things I was trying to do for myself. I would look up and see people around me getting attention, even if it was for all the wrong reasons. But to me, negative was better than none. I wanted someone to say, DeMarie, the sky is the limit. You are doing well, considering all you have been through thus far. Wandering further and further into the wilderness, Hope turned into heaviness. I have failed GOD so many times, no wonder He left me in the desert to die with a baby on my hip. My sins separated me from GOD. My hatred kept me from reading His word; I was tune deff. Completely cut off, I didn't have any more superpowers.

I wasn't hearing from Him and there were no visions to help guide me. I have gotten myself put out of Davine's house; I was used to it. The more I hung with Juvy, the more corrupt my life became. He was a magnet for trouble. My mom and sisters didn't like the energy he brought to my life. Hindsight, I was hit by a little white fat dude with a bow and arrow. No matter what this guy did, I was right by his side. The little DeMarie was in the house of my mind reminding me I was with this guy because that's what I thought I deserved! My body language attracted him along with the words Rodell and the world attached to me about being unworthy. Little DeMarie wants me to see that I was mixing up my files and making my life harder. Poor little DeMarie; she was being overworked.

I had artificial satisfaction from Juvy, so he would stay. I moved in with Dakota for a while, saved some money and got myself a place. I was still moving dope with the help of him and Eve. Eve was a breath of fresh air. I took an extra shift this day because I had so much clientele coming through my blow-up phone, Juvy had to manage it. "Drop me off at work and come pick me up at 6am." When he dropped me off, he had a friend who was going to braid his hair. I wasn't a braider, so I didn't mind. The only thing I couldn't stand about him was he was a heavy beer drinker. I worried he would get my car taken, along with my weed, money, and drugs. At 5am, I was trying to get ahold of him to pick me up on time. I was exhausted after the dirt-ass head nurse gave all thirty-two residents laxatives before bed. I was pissed that it was 6am, and he was still not answering. Sandy offered me a ride home; I was grateful. Me being the very understanding person that I am, I assumed he was burnt out from all the running last night; besides all the drinking and smoking, I'm sure he did. I had a two-bedroom apartment. There was linoleum for a coat rack and shoes when you walk in. To the left was the hallway to the rooms, and to the right was the kitchen and living room. I was a new resident, so I didn't have any furniture. I had a television and a stand. Ahniyah and I had beds, and that was about it. This particular time my nephew, Maurice, came to stay with me. Eve dropped me off. I got my keys and opened the door to see a pair of pink slides that didn't belong to me. I headed to the left to follow my nose like Tucan Sam. Niyah was in her room, sound asleep. Maurice was in my bed, knocked out alone. The one thing I didn't want to believe was becoming apparent. Anger often comes when we feel afraid; it acts as a defense and shield for protection. It comes in times of hurt, rejection, confusion and powerlessness. My battery pack was dreadfully low, yet my heart rate was increasing speedily. My body's thermometer had broken. My heavy feet through the house should have woken somebody up. There was instant foaming at the mouth once I hit the corner to the living room. My eyes knew what to fixate on. Tremors took over me once I began to caterwaul. These PUNK ASS MUTHERFUCKERS GOT THE AUDACITY TO BE UNCLAD, IN MY FUCKING HOUSE! I kept a steel bat in my closet. The bum ass nigga and the bitch didn't even wake up while I was getting my bat. I was reaching anger blackout stages, stumbling back to my subjects. I was experiencing ringing in my ears while striking these idiots repeatedly. I started feeling a sense of satisfaction. The bat vibrates every time I connect; letting me know I was getting to the white meat. "WAKE THE FUCK UP BITCH! WHAT THE FUCK IS THIS DIRTY BITCH DOING IN MY HOUSE?" They immediately jumped up, looking like Adam and Eve when they ate the apple. I took the hood rats' clothes and threw them off the balcony. They both were trying to explain why they don't have clothes on. At this point, I wanted to kill. RedRUM MUTHERFUCKERS! I ran to the kitchen to grab a knife, but this negro was bold enough to hold me from behind. My nephew came and took the knife and picked me up off the floor. "Let me go; you are a Sucker for letting this shit happen in MY house!" I was losing my voice and my mind. "Maurice, put me the fuck down! Go in the back with Niyah!" Soon as he put me down, I smoothed out the wrinkles on my scrubs. I was pretending like I was calm. SHIT! I took off running and did a roundhouse kick to her head; she landed right by the TV. I grabbed her hair and banged it on the floor; I physically couldn't fight anymore. It was time for them to meet their maker. Juvy was acting like the bitch he is, defending this hoe by pulling me off her. I got enough strength in me to crawl to my gun! She moved out of my way and hid behind him. I continued to move toward my gun. He must have realized I was going for it; he wasn't quick enough. Right underneath the firearm was a picture of Ahniyah. Everything was in slow motion. In silence, I asked God to forgive me! I knew I must be temporarily insane for what I was about to do. BOOM! BOOM! BOOM! Cacophonous sounds came from my door saying "OPEN THE DOOR, IT'S THE POLICE!" I put the weapon back and proceeded to the door. "Saved by the door bitches!" The officer said he got a complaint about arguing and fighting. Before I could say anything, this dumb bitch said she was held against her will and just wanted her clothes to go home and the officer made sure that happened; I also made him leave. If you thought I left him ultimately, you thought wrong. I deserved someone like him, remember?

Eve wasn't a fan of my relationship; she was pissed I let him come back. I was getting calls from my runners saying she wasn't picking up, she would never show up to meet them, or she was shorting them on product. This was it; I wasn't about to keep letting people sabotage everything I had built. Plus, I was almost close to my first goal of buying a home. Eve's sister started leaving messages on my voicemail saying, "BITCH, HOW CAN YOU CALL YOURSELF MY SISTER'S FRIEND?" or "I AM PRESSING CHARGES ON YOU!" I acted like she never called; she never stated her real problem. Davine called me saying, "Girl, whatever you are doing, your ways are catching up to you! Tell Eve's sister you don't live here so she can stop stocking my house!" Now, Eve was calling me talking about a family emergency, and that she would be gone for the weekend. I didn't even get to ask what the fuck was up her sister's ass before she hung up! Since she will be gone, I was taking all joogs. Shit needed to change because she was acting funny. I cut my hours back at work to be on call, I took a call that I wouldn't normally take, I always stuck to familiar stomping grounds, etc., my greed and urgency went for it because of the large amount attached. Everything was as normal; I pulled up at the gas station, grabbed the money, went inside the store, put the goods in the bag and put the bag in the trash. I wouldn't say I liked to ride with that kind of money on me, so I headed to my safe. It was right before dusk. I preferred to go in daylight, so if something tends to happen, someone would be near. I didn't follow my script, but I didn't smell any danger in the air. Before I could get in my car, two people forced me down to the ground. "Get down on the ground and put your hands behind your back!" "What do you want from me?" "You know what we want." "Shut up talking to us and take us to the money, or we will pop you right here!" Scared to fucking death; I knew no amount of my plea was worth it. I had a little girl to take care of, so I did stall because I needed time to catch a voice, a distinctive walk, and or smell. The quieter I became, the more they spoke amongst each other. The robbers felt victorious and said, "This is payback for all the lives you have ruined!" with a southern accent. This person sounded like I've heard their voice before. The second robber argued with the first because he was talking too much. The first robber was waving his hand around while yelling, then I noticed he had a finger that was flimsy with gloves on. Immediately, I remembered meeting a family member of Eve's; he did have a southern accent, and he was missing a finger. I was putting two and two together and was blown the fuck away. Could it be that I've been set up? Nah! I tried to reason and process all the thoughts that led to my demise. The robbers dug a hole and made me put my face in the dirt, and knocked me unconscious from a blow to the back of my head. I woke up after dark, in the park face down. My car, phone, and gun were stolen. I walked down the street to my Aunt Sugar's house to call for a ride. I was so demeaned that I couldn't say a word to anyone. A cousin of mine was cleaning out Aunt Sugar's attic and gave me a box full of letters that I had written to Paige. The conflicting feelings of heartbreak and joy overwhelmed me. I was relieved of my anger toward Aunt Sugar; she was trying to protect my feelings. I went and gave her the biggest hug. Waiting on my ride, I had time to reflect. I asked God, "What was I supposed to learn from two congruent but contrasting experiences?" I had hit rock bottom at this point. How do I explain this loss? It then dawned on me that both Chicago and Eve showed up in my life as my embedded core beliefs and past trauma. I recalled denouncing my connection with God. I spoke out loud about starting a new system of beliefs, but how could I when the real work to diminish the ***Governing Thought Chains***

(***GTC***) had never been introduced? Naturally, those Chains of ***THORNS*** continued to show up in my life.

Abundance Mindset

Knowing there is plenty for everyone to eat (be successful) without hoarding food, knowledge, and wealth from others.

Example: Sharing your knowledge about wealth building because you know someone could benefit from it is not taking anything away from what you have on your plate of abundance.

3 STEPS to an abundance mindset

1. Pay close attention to the thoughts creating a poverty mindset by taking thirty minutes daily for stillness. Take a quiet ride without the radio, TV or cell phones; meditate solemnly. Increase according to your availability and likeness.
2. Take action to pinpoint these Chief Theory Thorns (CTTs) by leading a healthy lifestyle and detoxifying your body and mind, detoxifying your mind by not complaining for thirty days. Show nothing but gratitude for the present moment. Be of service to others positively and intentionally.

3. Set a conscious trend to shift the CTTs to abundance. Replacing the CTTs with positive words, thoughts, and emotions.

Repeat.

THORN NINE

At thirty years old, I started seeking clarity on WHO I was, WHERE I wanted to go in life, and HOW I could be of service—Pen Pad and Paper in hand; I started writing down my goals. My first goal was to open a twenty-four-hour daycare, so I broke down the plans to get me there. I started by enrolling in Highline Community College for Early Childhood Education, I bought myself a two thousand Chevy Impala, found a house with six rooms and two living rooms—a big yard with a two-story clubhouse and going through my core belief files, I shredded any that no longer served me. The church was the primary place I knew to gain clarity on WHO I am.

'I am single now, so I can focus on myself and my two kids. Yes, I have a son now. His name is Najee. He is three years old. I know. I know! You're wondering who his father is? You guessed it, Juvy! The rest of that part of my life deserves a book on its own. Everything is calm, relaxed, and collected in my world right now. It's almost too good to be true.'

My stepmom, Karen, called me hysterically as she hasn't been able to find a place; she was being put out of her home. I wasn't quick to respond to her but when I did, I let her know only under the pretense that she won't tell her son La Donis (the monster) where I lived, and she agreed. I loved Momma Karen and felt like it was my obligation to help her because she had always been there for my kids and I. It was great. Momma Karen would usually cook dinner, we watched movies together and we went to every thrift store in town. One month had passed, and it was time to collect her rent. She explained that she would pay as soon as her check came, but I wasn't tripping at all. I always ensured I could handle my business, with or without help.

Momma Karen was not coming home these days and it got me feeling some kind of way because she never answered her phone. It has been five weeks that I haven't set an eye on her but I know she comes around. She was leaving her cigarette burning or leaving the TV going; all these to avoid paying me. I didn't want to involve my siblings, but somebody needed to tell me where this lady was. She did have a boyfriend whose house she would frequent. I just let it go for the time being. I wanted to believe she would pay me eventually. My main focus was school, work, and my kids. I worked part-time at Chevron, my hours were two o'clock pm until eleven o'clock at night. On this fateful day, I pulled up to my driveway and saw Momma's car. I finally caught up with her, but I was extremely exhausted; I had to get my kids in bed, I also had some studying to do. I opted to speak to her later because I knew I wouldn't last with my studies if I smoked the blunt I had waiting for me. With my face planted in my book, I was awakened by the familiar aroma of weed. Momma Karen doesn't smoke, but her man does. Feeling revived, I wanted to join the session. "Momma! Momma. Tell Smitty to let me smoke with him!" I wasn't getting a response. I assumed they can't hear me, or were asleep. As soon as I got to the staircase that led to the bottom floor, my body's alarm was going off. Siren sounds consumed my body. If humans didn't feel fear, we wouldn't be able to ward off physical or emotional danger. This part of my life was restored due to my reconnection to my Belief in GOD. My beliefs are connected to my first mind (my gut); it was there intuition brewed. A premonition was what caused the alarm to sound. People are wired to treat anything menacing as a threat to our well-being. As our internal alarm clock screams at us, it signals the brain to fight flight or freeze. An accelerated breathing rate caused my feet to grow roots and my calls for Momma turned into a whisper. At that moment, my superego yelled at me to run. . A quirky voice and cold hand grabbed my ankle and said, "Where are you going? I came to smoke with you." My anger shielded my fear. "GET THE FUCK OFF ME! GET OUT OF MY GOTDAMN HOUSE NOW! IF YOU DON'T LEAVE, I'M GOING TO KILL YOU!" My voice was raspy from yelling. The monster came up my stairs while I ran to the kitchen to grab a knife. My kids woke and stood at the top of the stairs. Ahniyah was screaming to leave her mommy alone. "Ahniyah, go get my phone and call nine one one." His hunchback, slew-footed creepy ass slithered away out my side door downstairs. I packed my shit and went to Paige's house. I found out from my step-sister, Leena, that she and Momma were in LAS VEGAS, kicking it. I was Livid. How could she go out of town without paying me my rent? She had the nerve to give this nigga keys to my house to come in whenever he pleases? At the time, I was like 'bitch get your shit out of my house'. After all, I've been through with her son, you let him have keys to my house to rape me or one of my kids. I can't understand the depths of the mental torture I have been subjected to in my life. Blunt after blunt after blunt. It was the only way I knew to suppress what has happened to me throughout life. My unyielding credence in GOD didn't waver this time, it caused me to search for a closer walk. My surroundings would go back to the normal dysfunction it's always been.

I was working religiously to complete my goals. Somehow it kept me busy, so I didn't have to address the thousands of words floating through my mind. I received a phone call from my Aunty Charity; she is one of my mom's younger siblings. "Hey, Aunty, How are you doing?" "Hey, DeMarie, how are you?" "Good." "Ok! Could you consider coming to my Momma's (my granny) house and take care of Granny (Great Granny)?" Before I could respond, she went on a tangent. "I'm out of town right now." Let me give you a little background on the situation. I have been going over to Momma's house every couple of hours to check on my grandmother; between work and school. It saddens me to see all the capable young people in my Momma's house not doing right by her or her mother. I went over there one day and noticed that my grandma had a swollen leg. She had to be rushed to Valley Medical Center in Renton, WA. It turned out she had a blood clot; that shit could have killed her. You already know I was in there going off. She didn't have to say much more. She let me know that she first reached out to Dakota to see if she could assist Granny and Great Granny but Dakota wasn't available, so she told Aunty to try me. At first, I didn't know if I was doing the right thing by quitting my job and giving up school. My final decision was solely based on the fact. My Great Granny Irene was as close to perfection as I had ever seen. Granny Irene had the odds stacked against her from Birth. She was born a twin on 27th September, 1916. They both had Polio, but her twin didn't make it. I don't know their age, but they were old enough for Granny Irene to remember her. A nurse took it upon herself to nurture my Great Granny back to health. My family's history had holes and gaps in it, I needed to say that because we never knew much about her life before traveling from Tennessee to Portland, Organ. She traveled from Tennessee to Portland, Organ, because she had a brother named Vincent who resided there. She did travel with a husband and one daughter, My Granny Faye. They moved from Portland, Organ, to Seattle, WA. From there, my Great Granny would go on to be one of the first African American Nurses in Seattle. My Granny Faye built a family she didn't get to experience growing up. Being the only child had to be lonely. She would have ten beautiful children, but one passed away from mental health complications. She also had a set of twins. As my Great Granny worked long hours to support her growing family, Granny Faye was getting comfortable with the Seattle nightlife. Many stars whom she knew personally would come and do shows. I heard she was a good mom until she started partying. It got so bad that Great Granny Irene had to pick up some of her grandchildren from the foster homes; in some cases, the police dropped them off. Struggling to take care of her grandchildren, good friends and neighbors would step in and help her out so she could keep her job. I believed Granny Faye held some deep-rooted resentment toward Great Granny Irene.

Something happened back in Tennessee; that is my hypothesis. I also heard that my Grandpa Oscar raped one of my eldest Aunties. I believed this added to the resentment she had for her mother. Certain things Granny Faye did, made this possible for me to feel this way. Granny Irene gave Granny Faye everything she could ever want. If she needed anything, her mother was there to assist. Granny Irene was a humble GOD-FEARING woman; she spent most of her free time at church. She had one hundred percent *Belief* in GOD and *JESUS*. Granny Irene understood the formula to have a well-put-together plan. Her plans included leaving trust funds and safe deposit boxes to her daughter and nine grandchildren. Great Granny Irene owned her own three-story home, she had life insurance for her whole family and she was very meticulous about the way she spent money. Even though Granny Irene was almost flawless, the question remains, "Why did she stay with Grandpa Oscar after such accusations?"

At some point in our timeline in 1982, DeMarie was born. After Poppa got custody of me, Granny Irene would help him. I loved going to her house. She wouldn't give me candy as most Grandma's do, but she would let me pick blackberries in her backyard. The blackberries were for her succulent pies. I always helped her make it on Sundays. I could stay up late and watch wrestling and the best part was I got to eat ice cream too, which became a ritual of ours. Granny Irene would take me to get my hair washed and pressed at the shop. I don't recall her ever raising her voice at me, even if I broke one of her collectible salt and pepper shakers. She had shakers from all over the world, some are even worth money. They sat neatly and always shining and sparkling inside a beautiful china cabinet; it was hard not to touch one. I never got yelled at for going upstairs to slide down the rail, even after she told me not to. Unconditional love was what she always showed to everyone. She never turned Rodell down when it came to me.

Granny Irene was approaching old age; she was in her seventies when she took a fall, a fall that would forever change her life. Granny Faye took that fall as a means to control her mother's well-being and estate. She tricked her mother into signing papers that gave her power of attorney over her, and before Granny Irene knew it, she was being uprooted from all she had built. Granny Faye snatched her mom away from her friends and church family, she also moved her mom in with her and sold her mom's home without her permission. Granny Irene's house was sold for less than the actual market value, and this got her devastated. She loved her only child, but my Granny Faye lived a fast life compared to hers. Granny Irene didn't want any parts of it; she didn't complain. Although her ***Belief, Faith and Hope*** in ***God*** and ***Jesus*** were truly being put through the inferno. Granny Faye took care of her mom; I know that she loved her mom so much. However, at times it seemed like she was burdening her daughter. Granny Irene was more than self-sufficient. Over the years, she was starting to decline in some ways. For all those reasons stated, I wholeheartedly felt I owed it to her to be there for her.

On my first day on the job; I remembered at the time Granny Irene was ninety-five, I walked into the back room and met her in a gloomy atmosphere. No pictures on the walls, no open curtains, and her room had not been cleaned in a while. I found balls of feces hard as a rock underneath her bed, then I went further to examine her and noticed her right leg was starting to retract.

My hours are from seven in the morning to seven at night. Although I had long hours, but the people living around were responsible for her well-being the rest of the time. I always wrote down things I found needed to be completed. During the day, I would move her around her room so she could look out the window, disinfecting and sterilizing as we sang Christian songs and listened to the word on television. I slowly gave her a reason to still have ***Hope*** in a ***belief system*** that has never failed her. If any family would come over, including me beforehand, Granny Faye made sure people would go and speak to her. Although Granny Faye got to the point where she couldn't physically care for her mother, her voice was strong enough to demand help. People like Davine and Keyma were coming around regularly to keep Granny Irene's hair done. I also had a boy cousin named Rich; he loved her to pieces. He would make sure she was fed always. They ate yogurt, read the Bible, prayed, and sang gospel songs even at night. He loved on her so hard that she would put him out of her room. Rich and most of the cousins had some heavy problems with drug use. Nobody who lived there wanted to be responsible for her. At least seven to ten people over thirteen lived there consistently, not including my two grandmothers. Rich did all he could and even when he wasn't in his right mind, he knew to care for her. If nobody else was willing to help my Granny Faye bathe her mom, he would volunteer to do that. We have way too many people in my family for there not to be more of a rotation. If you were coming around to visit, as I would alone with other family members. It appeared all her affairs were handled because everyone was living there. The problem with all those people there was that everyone comes and goes as they please. Why didn't she have a caregiver before me, you say? She did. Granny Faye didn't want just anyone working there, this was most likely because of all the crazy stuff happening in her home.

After the third day, I noticed that Granny Irene was soaking wet from her neck down to her feet. In my mind, I was thinking; I know, goddamn well, she can't be wetting herself that much. If everyone was doing what I asked, she should be changed and rotated between three to five times a night. I wanted to check myself first but I had to make sure I wasn't tripping. Before I left that night, I marked Granny Irene's depend (diaper). Most of the time, I sat on the phone talking to my mom, Davine, and Dakota; on a three-way call discussing the daily zombie zoo happening at Granny Faye's house. I told them what I did and how anxious I was to get to work in the morning, and they assured me they were on standby if I needed anything.

I got to work an hour early. Not knowing what I was walking into, I braced myself. I honestly wanted them to do better; that's it! This time not only was she pissy from head to toe, her beautiful, long, salt and pepper hair was wet as well. I was ringing pee out of her hair. She was cold from having to lay in a wet nightgown all night.

I got to her depends; I was so fucking angry that I felt like popping a blood vessel. Great Granny Irene had on the same depend (diaper) since seven o'clock the night before. I couldn't wait to give these sorry mother fucking people a piece of my mind. Everybody got the nerve to be asleep. Oh, I was going to give Granny Faye a piece of my mind too. She wasn't getting off my shit list that easy. I cleaned Granny Irene up and prepared her breakfast, picked her up and put her in her wheelchair and then took her to the living room so she can hear me cuss these fools out;I snapped. The first person close to me was Granny Faye. Instead of sleeping in her room, she found herself on the couch. I understood she wasn't capable of caring for her physically, but again she could use her voice; her voice shoots daggers. Nobody messed with Granny Faye; she played no games. "Granny! Why every morning I come over here, your mom is soaking wet? Huh? It doesn't make any fucking sense you got all these folks up in your house. Everyone is too lazy to get their ass up to tend to Great Granny. Twelve mother fucking hours! Twelve fucking hours!" The more I thought about it, the more my muscles tensed. I was feeling flushed in the face. Granny Faye was asking me not to holler at her. At that moment, I realized I shouldn't have yelled at her because she is still my Granny. Now the dead were beginning to awake. Nobody could appreciate my tone, let alone my message instead they all started attacking me with their words. I was walking around the house, clapping my hands in between words, still yelling.

My uncle and his girlfriend came out of the garage talking shit to me too; it was so many of them against me, it was crazy. Even Granny Faye had got her little short self off the couch now that she had backups. I was ready for war at this moment and would go in on anyone of these crazy people who tries to swing on me. They forgot that I wasn't alone at the end of the day.

I went outside and sat in my car, called Dakota and then broke down in tears. I thanked GOD for her and her prayers. I was all alone in that house of darkness. My family was allowing drugs to take over. Half of them didn't know if they were coming or going. I believed we did things to open the gate for the ID in our house of consciousness to take over the host, just like a parasite would. Nonetheless, I loved them with all my heart. I had a different understanding of who or what was controlling them; Davine was at work. In a flash, I remembered Davine, Dakota, and Paige coming to have my back and set some shit straight.

Oh, everyone was quiet then. I would later learn that they all felt entitled to the money I was making, including Granny Faye. She approached me one day, saying she should be paid too because she helps take care of her mom too. I couldn't believe my ears. How could you feel you need to be paid to care for your mom? Every day I pulled up to that house, there exist this burden I couldn't describe. Dakota had to pray with me every morning.

Those guys were stealing money from Granny Faye; breaking into her room, stealing things under her nose. The house was full of pandemonium. The very ones she favored were turning on her. I felt there was favoritism over the years. Growing up, Granny Faye never ever had pictures of Paige and her kids or our kids. She operated differently with my siblings growing up. Paige, Ivonne, Davine, Dakota, and DeMarie didn't get the same treatment or reaction from her as the others. All of us have unique life experiences to tell.

Although Granny Faye can be a cold-hearted woman, but she raised so many of the neighborhood kids. She was a pillar in her community. As she got older, she began to change her ways. She didn't cuss like a sailor anymore, rather she was going to church and living a humble life.

It was Granny Faye's Birthday on March 14th; she was born in 1933. The Wright family loved a reason to come together. We may have dysfunctions, we may fight and fuss, but we always looked forward to a good party. A party where Granny Faye always stood as the Domino Queen. Uncle Andrew (drew) was always on the grill. Granny Faye had the best sound system. We kept the blunts rotating and the alcohol flowing. Even Great Granny was in the living room enjoying herself; she was able to have a wine cooler. The doctors who came to see her said to give her what she wanted. Another Uncle by the name of K showed up, he brought Granny Faye her own bottle of liquor and also poured her a drink. Although she was already drinking before he got there. After a while, she got up to go to the bathroom then we heard a loud thud; Granny Faye fell. She kept telling us she was fine and insisted on not opening the door. Uncle K kicked the door in and found Granny Faye on the floor with a giant knot on her head. She yelled at us to leave her alone, insisting she didn't want to be admitted.

Granny summoned me to the couch to discuss how she could get some of the money; it was a simple no for me. I was bussing my butt to take care of Great Granny, so why should I have to share my earnings? This little lady had the nerve to fire me, she was literally on her way to the hospital. She also was complaining about me being late some days, which was true because it was dreadful coming to her house; I was never certain what to expect. Most days, it was so bad I stayed in the room with Great Granny Irene.

I was sitting in my car crying as Granny Faye was being picked up by the ambulance. I went home, took a shower to wash off all the pain from the trial I was up against. All I wanted to do was give Great Granny the support she deserved. How does she continue to have Faith and Hope in a God that stripped her of everything, including being able to worship Him? Why does she continue to find comfort in Jesus? Will she be okay without me? I was even sadder for Granny Faye because she was a Matriarch of the family. We never wrapped our minds around her ever being sick or hurt enough to need an ambulance ride.

Paige called me in the middle of the night. I looked at the phone, unwilling to answer. The Wright's family were been traumatized by late-night calls. I felt it in my bones that something wasn't right as Paige and others kept calling. While going through all the things in my mind that could be the problem, I cut my ringer off. I decided not to answer anyone. Then I noticed my mom at my door. "DeMarie, why aren't you picking up? Momma is being kept at the hospital. She is bleeding internally. The team of Doctors is running all kinds of tests." "Wait, What!" I ran around the house frantically trying to pack a bag.

The Wright family wasn't mentally prepared for Granny Faye to be sick; it turned out my Granny had a cancerous tumor. The Doctors told us she could undergo chemo to shrink the tumor and they believed she had an estimated ten years if she was willing to go through with it. Granny Faye refused her treatment; she was tired. The family members she loved the most were sucking her dry. She was behind on the most important bills; rent, lights, phone, her mom's two storages full of all her antiques and family history. I think she was confused as to what was happening to her. I honestly think she didn't know these drug addicts were robbing her blind. Some of them had the nerve to be in her house, fighting with her about helping with their food stamps and paying her Rent for staying there. She has always been a hustler; she always made a way to keep up with her bills. She was getting older. If she had reached out to one of her kids and told them what was happening, we could have gotten together and helped her pay her past-due bills. When we all found out about her mother's storage, it was too late.

While she was in the hospital, she asked for her mom. This prompted the family to urge me to bring Great Granny Irene to the hospital to see her but I clearly got my stubbornness from Granny Faye because I was hell-bent on not bringing her. On the flip side, although I've been fired, I'm still on paper. So, I humbled myself and took Great Granny to see her daughter. Granny Faye first says, "Wow, she is doing better than me!" Great Granny Irene was very alert and carried an illuminating light like no other. Granny Irene didn't understand what was going on and My Granny

Faye couldn't comprehend where most of her favorites were at; she was constantly asking for them. Damn the ones who were mistreated the most, being by her side. She wanted Keema and so many others who couldn't be available for her, but those were the ones losing their minds, literally.

Granny Faye was so stubborn that she could barely look at me. Her last words to me were, "Do you have a new job yet?" I responded with a humble 'No'. She didn't ask me to come back or apologize in any way. Moreover, I didn't care at this point, even though it hurt. I know my grandmother. I promised God that I wouldn't leave Great Granny's side. I also wasn't about to fight with anyone regarding her well-being. Granny must have talked with GOD; it felt like she was done with this world.

Dakota got in touch with an Aunt of ours who chose not to be around the family for her own reasons. She usually come around to help the rest of her siblings sort things out with their mom. She brought Granny Faye home for the first time since she fell on her birthday. I will never forget the look on her face when she walked through the door; Granny Faye looked around in confusion. "Where am I?" she said,

"Please take me back to the hospital." It was hard watching her bewilderment. My aunty had to take her to the bank to see about getting her bills paid. Within three months, the family was in rotation to never leave her alone at the hospital.

THORN TEN

Granny was declining rapidly, she wasn't eating or drinking. The time came for her to be moved to Hospice where she would take her final breath. All our family was here. She had six generations surrounding her, blessing her transition. I was away at Walmart with one of my aunts by the time she was about to take her last breath. Two people were the closest to her; Dakota and Rich. A family tree of six generations became five. Some of the families that lost their minds never got them back. The hospital she was at took excellent care of her. It was time for us all to go, but go where? We were ALL lost at this time. The Wright family had to put together fundraisers. Granny lapsed on her insurance to keep her mother's life insurance because she obviously thought she would outlive her mother and not the other way around. I continued to go to Granny's house to care for her mom. I never will understand why families fight when someone dies. An unruly atmosphere was settling around us, so I tried my best to stay in the back room with Great Granny since we had a broken window in the front of the house. My uncle and one of my cousins were fighting and chasing each other down the street with weapons. I kid you not, so many fights broke out during the whole process of raising funds for Granny Faye. While all this was going on, my Granny Faye was being evicted; she resided in that home for twenty-plus years. The owners were ready to start the eviction process as soon as they heard she was sick, which was coming to fruition. Some of these family members were so numb that they weren't even trying to find a new place to live. People were ready to start cleaning out my Granny's belongings and taking what they wanted. We got to the attic and out came a chest full of pictures. For a second, we were all unified while laughing at baby pictures of my aunts and uncles. I found pictures of people on my dad's side of the family too; all the pictures of Paige growing up, her kids, and grandkids were here. It was bittersweet. I always wondered what she was doing with our photos. It was time to close the chapter on this part of our lives. How will we all move forward and still be a unit? We don't; so much hurt was caused during this transition. Some siblings still don't speak to this day. Struggling to figure out what would happen to Great Granny Irene, I offered to take her into my home since I already cared for her. I moved out of that big home I was living in. After my mom and her siblings agreed she was best with me, she moved in. I gave her Najee's room and moved into my new place way before she would come live with me. My house was on a hill all by itself.

The driveway was on a hill too. My new assignment began; I began to fall into a deep depression. The house we lived in was set apart from everyone else's and the world, I called it my little Island. All I had was time; time to overthink and time to spend with myself. I didn't realize there would come a time when I would need help. Paige, Davine, and Dakota were the only ones who showed up when it mattered most. My kids' birthdays would pass. The family said they would show up to care for Great Granny so that I could celebrate with them. We would get dressed and ready but nobody ever showed up. I was sacrificing, and so were my two little ones. No summer vacations or outings. We couldn't even walk to the corner store. I was not one to complain because I knew the totality of what I was doing. I had been a care provider since the age of sixteen; I had seen it all. The crying out for help started to fade. I believed some of the siblings were operating in greed. Great Granny had life insurance that was paid through her retirement money. My Aunt who came back around before her mom passed. In the quest to figure out a way to gain a higher power of GUARDIAN ADLIGHTEM, one of her siblings was trying to take Granny from my home, pushing a narrative that she had the power of attorney when she didn't. My Aunt with the GA offered it to me, but I said 'no' as I am just the great-granddaughter. I knew there was life insurance to be dispersed one day but I wanted no part of that. If the Wright family fell apart when no life insurance was present, I could only imagine what it would be like this time around. I was grateful for her. She acted as Granny's voice and got all her affairs in order.

I was beginning to feel overwhelmed, shut in, and shut out. Sometimes I would get us all dressed for church, and the stupid access van would never show up. My ***Faith*** was slowly being depleted. My ***Hope*** was on low battery. Granny Irene's plethora of appointments was becoming difficult to maintain. The van meant to pick us up stopped coming to get us because of where I was located. I was completely broken down, lower than a pregnant ant's stomach. I was starting to drink every day. Out of the many prayers I prayed, one got through. I prayed for knowledge, something I have never done. The knowledge came in the form of a book; it was dropped off on my front porch by someone unknown to this day. THE SECRET by *RHONDA BYRNE*. I always compared anything I read to the word of GOD. It was a direct download from GOD. God also gave me a song of praise to keep with me on this journey. *KIERRA SHEARD "You Don't Know" Through restoring my* ***Hope***. GOD gave me a dream that I have had since I was a child. My view was ascending from what felt like the heavens. I could only see a thick book falling from the sky onto my doorstep. All my life, I had been told to write my story. Many times so far, I tried. Pruning was in process for me. I couldn't fully get this story out. GOD would put me through something and say, "***NOW WRITE***!"

I stayed on my knees, explaining and pleading to Him and giving His word back to Him about everything He promised me. That was the only request I genuinely sought to get me off this hill so we all could have a better quality of life. But I was unlucky. I broke down going to look at a potential house, but the tenth house owner called to tell me they were going with another family; even when they understood my situation. Coming down a hill, all I remembered was crying my eyes out. I couldn't see a thing but a dead-end street. I turned down this road and pulled over, shouting, crying, and yelling cuss words. Feeling lost and lonely, I sat in my car ready to take my own life. I was failing my grandmother. I would have to tell my Aunt I couldn't do it anymore. I made a promise to GOD, so I would ride this wave until He called her home. The shit wasn't working, so I took it as a sign she wasn't supposed to be with me. I got out of the car and smoked a blunt. I looked up; there was a house in front of me with a 'For Rent' sign in the window. The owner happened to be outside. GOD said, "Talk to him." Being a timid person, I had to be looking crazy because I was literally going back and forth with myself. With faith the size of a mustard seed; I did it! "Hello, Sir! I see your house is for rent?" he climbed down the ladder. "I'm sorry it has been rented. I was going to take it out the window soon. Can I have your number? If it doesn't work, I will give you a call." "Thank you, Sir!" as I turned and walk away. I trust you, GOD. I went back to my Island defeated. All I had was ***Faith***, the size of a mustard seed. If anything else happened, I was going to end it all. GOD wasn't done with me yet. Two weeks later, I got the call. The owner of the last house I saw was willing to meet with me and start getting me into the house. I didn't have to do a background check. I told him my story, and he was moved. I'm forever grateful for this house; I still live in it as I write this testimony.

The next six years were much easier when GOD told me to bring Dakota on since I had a vacant house next door. I told her to see about the house; she got in afterward. GOD is doing some amazing things. HE'S been hearing me all alone. HIS timing is like none other; always on time. I could be falling from a cliff, and GOD will swoop me up right before I hit the ground. It was just a small few that would come and visit Great Granny and sit with her so we can have a break. Dakota and her unwavering faith were the balance we needed. I watched this girl transform into an eagle metaphorically. We did all we could to keep Granny happy and comfortable. I worked twenty-four hours a day, so I had to go back to my day job at Chevron to enable me stay up all night with Granny. I NEVER missed a beat. I knew Granny Faye, and GOD was watching me. I wanted them to be so proud of me. Granny Irene didn't know us personally anymore. She knew we were family, but that was it. How was it that she could remember GOD and JESUS? Dakota and I had a habit of asking her what she was doing when she was in complete silence, she would say she was praying. She is a woman they SAID had Dementia. A woman they SAID had to be on warfarin (blood-thinner), but as it turned out it was killing her, I had them take her off it. She proved she could live without it. This lady would continue to be an active miracle.

When the time came for me to change Granny and feed her some late-night snacks, I saw a lump in her breast. I called Dakota and my aunt with the GA. We had to rush her to the emergency room. I also called all the family so we could pull together for her. The whole Wright family took shifts as we did with
Granny Faye. I remembered the doctors had a meeting on this day. They told us it was about to be over. Great Granny was asking us to buy her ***Roses.*** She was under meds. Her request was, "***Give me Roses while I can smell them.***" So we did. We had a 'Do Not Resuscitate'. Granny was too frail to be done that way. She was sent home to be comforted with hospice care. The worldly doctors couldn't do anything more for her. The lump in her breast was discolored and hot to the touch. Out of nowhere, her lump was gone. Her doctors and nurses couldn't believe what was happening. They had never seen anything like it. Granny never complained about being in pain. All she would say is, "The

LORD is helping me." Never once did she tell the nurse she was in pain.

Granny was been rushed back to the hospital again when a lump was spotted forming again. As a family, we knew GOD was our doctor. Once again; scared, but believing what GOD was telling and showing us was a Miracle for sure. We went on with our lives and I have since been married and now pregnant. In March 2017, heavily pregnant me was up because there was a very foul smell coming from her room, plus it was also time to do my normal check-ins with her to ensure she was being rotated and relieved of pressure points. Thank GOD for my daughter and son, they were always helping me with her. My husband also treated her as his own. I pulled the blankets back but couldn't process what was going on. There was blood everywhere. It literally smelt like death. By this time, Granny had anxiety. She was eating her hands and was fidgeting heavily. Dakota and I wondered if the end was really near this time. She was sleeping less and less. We called family, telling them the end was near, to come see her. Not many people would come to see her.

We didn't care though. Another trip to the hospital would make it the third time we were there. ALL PRAISED TO THE MOST HIGH. He was showing us all to have ***Faith*** in Him. After a week, we were home again. Eventually, Granny stopped bleeding. There was so much blood, y'all, there was no way she was still alive. At the time, she was ninety-nine years old and weighs about 90 pounds soaking wet. Her anxiety grew. She was staring off in the corners of the room like she saw something or someone. On May 27th, I woke up gasping for air. I felt my Granny slipping away. I called Dakota, but she couldn't be there at the time. My husband and daughter were so worried about me, considering I was eight months pregnant. I wanted so bad for her to meet her granddaughter. GOD had other plans that day. The three of us watched as Granny's body was glitching. My husband was reading the Bible to her, helping her transition. I could feel her body turning cold. I looked into her eyes and saw her spirit exit her body through her mouth. Soon after, we witnessed something remarkable; a smile. I knew something she saw on the other side made her happy. Devastation took over me, then I started to scream.

What am I going to do without her? How was I supposed to go on? Dakota was rushing to be by my side. We kept her body as long as we could until it was time to let the funeral home pick her up. In the midst of all of this, we found out Granny didn't have but a three-thousand-dollar policy. GOD wasn't done with us yet. The argument would start again between the sisters about what to do with her. My aunt with the GA wanted to make sure my sister and I had some say-so over her arrangements and services. It looked like all she could afford was a cremation. My Aunty Charity started to do the footwork as she was hell-bent on not cremating Granny. Honestly, that wasn't what Granny would have wanted. She then discovered that Granny Irene had a plot right next to her husband. After many private conversations between Dakota and I, we understood Great Granny Irene passed her mantle down to us to continue to be the LIGHT for our family, never to forget whose lineage we came from, and to always keep our core belief in GOD alive. She taught us to be humble, and no matter what, wait on JESUS because without Him, you can't get to GOD.

God showed me throughout my life that He was with me, even when situations arose to break me. I never fully gave up on my belief system, though it wavered but never failed. With my whole heart, I knew if He had saved me from so much there was no way I could lose my ***Faith***. Every day with Granny Irene was a lesson on **Belief**, **Faith, Hope**, and ***Mindset***.

Every single little thing was to prepare me to care for Great Granny. GOD pruned me, molded me, and tested the depths of my loyalty to Him. Would I fold under pressure? Would I continue to be timid? He turned this cowardly lion into an Alpha Woman. GOD knew just what I needed. Having a ***Positive Core Belief System*** mixed with an ***Abundance Mindset***, ***Faith***, and ***Hope*** is important. ***Faith*** in yourself and what isn't tangible, ***Hope*** that all things good will come, and the right ***Mindset*** to make it all possible. I am a living testimony of what can happen if you ground yourself with these five words, no matter the *Thorns*. The thorns will come at a point in your life and when it does, use these tools to take yourself away from them to the Throne of Abundance.

"IF YOU WANT THE MOON, DO NOT HIDE AT NIGHT. IF YOU WANT A ROSE, DO NOT RUN FROM THE THORNZ. IF YOU WANT LOVE, DO NOT HIDE FROM YOURSELF." ~RUMI

Have you ever felt like you were in the eye of a storm? No matter what you do, that storm grows and feeds off what I call *CHIEF THEORY THORNS (C.T.T.) when* you only want to quiet the storm. I have put together the first steps to get you from the *THORNS* in your world to the *THRONE* that is rightfully yours. Your THRONE awaits you to take total control over your inner matrix. I gave you my unique life experiences to show you what the absence and presence of ***ABUNDANCE MINDSET, BELIEF, FAITH,*** AND ***HOPE*** looked like through my cognizance. These words, in part with action, are the building blocks to your foundation of *THE HOUSE OF CONSCIOUSNESS.* ***ABUNDANCE MINDSET, BELIEF, FAITH,*** *AND* ***HOPE*** aren't something you have; they are created and instilled. Having ***AM.B.F.H*** doesn't mean you won't have any storms to overcome. ***AM.B.F.H*** are there to change the frequency of your thoughts about the storm. Once you have shifted to awareness, your brain can sort the experience, ideas, and feelings attached. Please understand YOU MUST DO YOUR SELF WORK, BE HONEST WITH THE ID, SUPEREGO, and EGO (yourself). It will never change overnight. Having an ***AM.B.F.H*** are things to work on daily. I can only speak from my personal experience. My most significant building block was the ***CORE BELIEF IN GOD. GOD*** was first installed in me through my parents' ***BELIEF SYSTEM*** (download). My life experiences tested my ***BELIEF, FAITH, and HOPE*** in all I depended on, ***GOD.***, which took me through the eye of many storms that brought me full circle to THE MOST HIGH GOD. Conditioning your ***AM.B.F.H*** by being around like-minded being, reading positive books, self-affirmations, and meditation (stillness) are the keys to ***AM.B.F.H.*** Doing this helps to diminish the thorns that are constantly popping up and pocking your mind, thereby causing your energy to give off low vibration and anxiety. A Nadir vibe signals to the universe, saying you deserve your storm or are searching for the eye of the storm. According to research, humans have about six thousand thoughts per

day—a median of about six thoughts per minute. Most ideas aren't connected to anything specific. Taking time to recognize the ***CHEIF THEORY THORNS (CTT)*** and shifting them to abundance will heighten your vibrations. The ***thorns*** in your life are here to cause fear, discomfort, and difficulty to your obstacles. I want to let you know you are already on track. Unconsciously, YOU attracted THIS ABUNDANCE OF KNOWLEDGE to yourself. So, keep going and show gratitude in EVERYTHING. I will leave you with one of my favorite quotes "WHEN THE STUDENT IS READY; THE TEACHER
WILL APPEAR" Lao Tzu. Now, go and bank on your truth.

EPILOGUE

Contrary to some people's beliefs, Paige consciously decided to get clean. She has been sober for twenty years plus. She is in the women's ministry in church, where she helped women who had similar experiences as hers. Davine is now a retired nurse who travels. She also owns properties. Dakota loves God more than anyone I know; she has started a ministry and often called to bring forth the word of God. As for Ivonne, he continued to have multiple setbacks in life. Unresolved childhood trauma would continue to ride him until he can be strong enough to master his thoughts. Ivonne is brilliant and wants to help young men to not go down some dark roads he took; I have hope in him. Mastering my mindset is a continuous terrain in my thirties;

those were the stories that I didn't tell. Once Great Granny Irene passed, I had to reposition myself. I reapplied the keys to refresh my perspective and moved to the next lessons in my life. The next level came with obstacles as well. I buried myself in work, helping my kids manage their clothing business, being a serial entrepreneur and preparing for "success" which was only possible through an abundance mindset, belief in my abilities, faith in myself and spiritual awareness, and hope that all things will happen for the greater of my good. I realized I was successful. Success to me is overcoming obstacles (thorns) that you never thought possible. For me, that is becoming an available wife and parent too, having multiple businesses, and being a prosperous Author. Most importantly, remembering not to get lost being a superhero... Mastering your mind is a lifelong journey, as you will continually evolve.

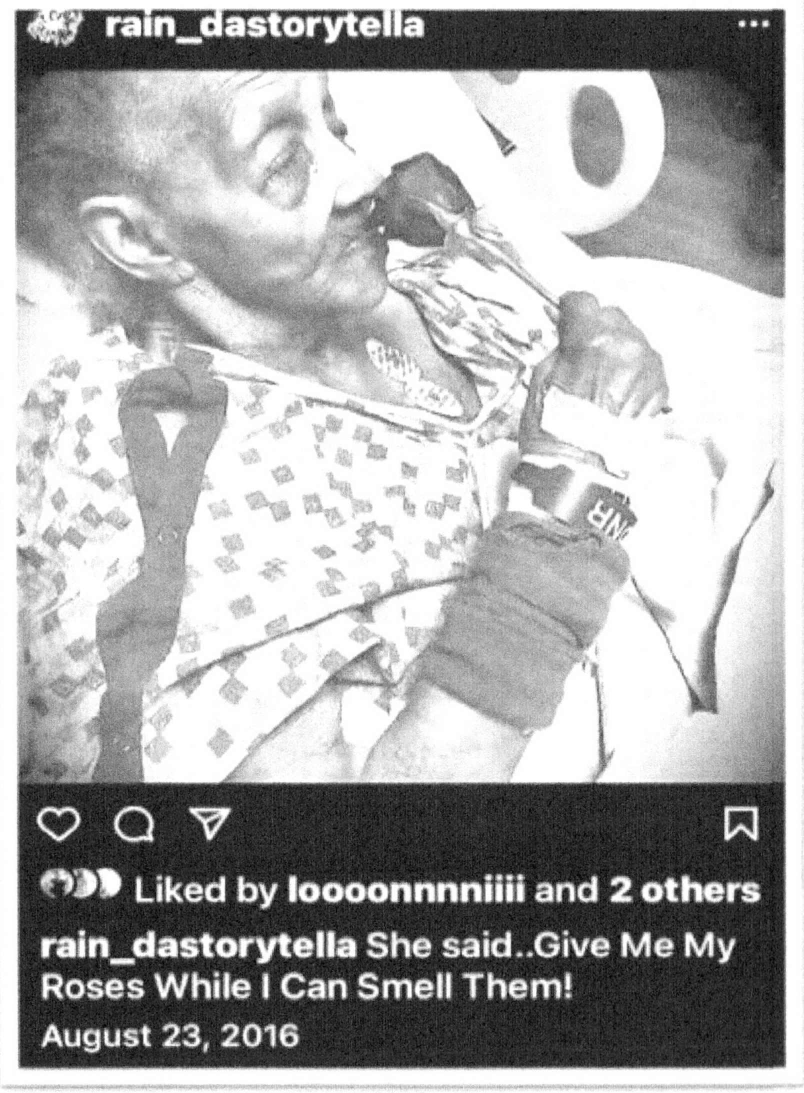
rain_dastorytella
Liked by loooonnnniiii and 2 others
rain_dastorytella She said..Give Me My Roses While I Can Smell Them!
August 23, 2016

ABOUT THE AUTHOR

Adell Austin, who goes by the pen name Rain The Truthteller (Rain) was born in Seattle, Washington. At the age of six, multiple people planted seeds in Rain that she had a story inside of her. Her love for reading and writing would nurture the talent given. Her passion was poetry and short stories throughout elementary, middle, and high school.

At the age of twenty-seven, Rain set her intention that she would be a published author. A journey of knowledge for the next thirteen years of conferences, webinars, mentorships, and self-study led Rain to be a successful author, motivational speaker, and coach.

When Rain isn't sitting in front of her laptop pumping out content, she is a serial entrepreneur who enjoys being a foodie, spending time with her family and friends, and appreciates her self-care days.

Made in the USA
Las Vegas, NV
29 April 2023

71312373R00138